*Andrea Livnat*

# 111 Places in Tel Aviv That You Shouldn't Miss

*Photographs by Angelika Baumgartner*

emons:

© Emons Verlag GmbH
All rights reserved
© Photographs by Angelika Baumgartner, except ch. 3: Dafna Gazit;
ch. 7, 13, 25, 42, 86, 100, 104, 105, 106: Andrea Livnat;
ch. 21 above: Ariel Ken; ch. 21 below: Inbal Hershtig;
ch. 28: Mauritius images / dov makabaw Israel / Alamy;
ch. 30: Arik Livnat; ch. 72: Daniel Lailah
© Cover motif: iStockphoto.com / julichka
Layout: Eva Kraskes, based on a design
by Lübbeke | Naumann | Thoben
Maps: altancicek.design, www.altancicek.de
Basic cartographical information from Openstreetmap,
© OpenStreetMap-Mitwirkende, ODbL
English translation: John Sykes
Copyediting: Rosalind Horton
Printing und binding: Lensing Druck GmbH & Co. KG,
Feldbachacker 16, 44149 Dortmund
Printed in Germany 2018
ISBN 978-3-7408-0263-9
First edition

Did you enjoy it? Do you want more?
Join us in uncovering new places around the world on:
www.111places.com

# Foreword

Tel Aviv was born from a dream. On 11 April, 1909, the 66 founding families assembled in the sand dunes north of Jaffa and drew lots for the plots of land on which they were to build their houses. They dreamed of a Jewish town without the cramped conditions of the city of Jaffa. Ahuzat Bait, 'home place', was their name for the first new district. A year later the name was changed to Tel Aviv – after the title of the Hebrew translation of Theodor Herzl's utopian novel *The Old New Land*. In this work Herzl, the founder of political Zionism, coined a memorable phrase: 'If you will it, it is no dream'.

The Scottish urban planner Sir Patrick Geddes designed a vision of a modern garden city. In 1925, he presented a comprehensive plan for Tel Aviv that included the essential characteristics of the main streets, residential districts and green spaces. Since then Tel Aviv has expanded in all directions, and some parts of the dream have become a nightmare. Today the city lives from its image as a place that never sleeps. High-tech, nightlife and Bauhaus style are its dominant features. Even though all of these clichés are true, there is so much more to discover!

Often known as the Big Orange, the White City by the sea is in many ways the epitome of innovation and plurality, but also often astonishingly provincial, orderly and family-friendly. Tel Aviv has few sightseeing classics, so those who want to get to know the city (even better) must walk its streets and go with the flow. These 111 places will help you to do this. While searching for them I fell in love with Tel Aviv all over again. On every corner, there awaits a surprise to quicken the pulse of a historian, to delight the eye of an art lover and to please the palate of a gourmet.

# 111 Places

# 1  The Abu Nabut Fountain

*A relic of Jaffa's golden age*

There is a small domed Islamic building on Ben Zvi Street. Sabil Abu Nabut is a public fountain that was built in the early 19th century by order of the governor of Jaffa. Abu Nabut, who was actually called Mahmud Aga and was appointed to his office after the end of the Napoleonic invasion, had a reputation for being a strict ruler. He took his name from the stick (Nabut) that he always carried with him as a weapon and was accustomed to using without warning. At the same time, however, he was responsible for many important acts of modernisation in Jaffa. He restored the city walls and established new markets, as well as building mosques and two public fountains. Sabil Abu Nabut was outside the city on the route to Ramle and Lod, which continued to Jerusalem, and is mentioned in the reports of many 19th-century travellers as a small oasis by the roadside.

The city government of Tel Aviv has unfortunately made little effort to preserve and restore this unique structure. This is apparent from the lack of care devoted to the plaque on the façade, which wrongly dates it to 1820–21. In fact, the Arabic inscription states that it was built in the year 1230 of the Islamic calendar, i.e. in 1815 CE.

The rectangular building with three domes and little turrets at the corners housed tombs. The fountain itself was on the west façade. Today the windows of the tombs have been walled up, and the middle space is a junk room, used for storing equipment. Archaeological reports from the 19th century mention the existence of Abu Nabut's grave in the immediate vicinity. It disappeared in the 1950s. In its place the city government has used the open space next to it to lay out a small park with colourful sculptures by the Israeli artist Igael Tumarkin, which look strangely unnatural when seen next to the traditional architecture.

**Address** Abu Nabut Garden, Derech Ben Zvi, between Shlabim and Herzl Street,
Tel Aviv – Herzl hill (Givat Herzl)/Tel Kabir | Getting there Bus 11 to Derech Ben
Zvi/Herzl, in the opposite direction Machon haRishui/Derech Ben Zvi, bus 3, 72 to
haGan hazoologi/Herzl, in the opposite direction Derech Ben Zvi/Herzl | Hours
Accessible 24 hours | Tip If you walk a little way north on Shlabim Street you come to the
Groningen Garden, where there is a municipal music school. In front of it is one of the city's
strangest playgrounds with electronic toys that make a terrible noise but delight children.

# 2 The Afeka Caves

*Tel Aviv's green backyard*

Drezner Street, in Ramat Aviv Gimmel in the far north of the city, is nothing out of the ordinary. Between pleasant detached family homes close to the crossroads with Gruner Street you can go about 200 metres further north through an uninviting gap in the buildings. You have to struggle through – it's a spot where the local dogs leave their traces – to be rewarded with an unexpected view. This is where the city suddenly comes to an end: beyond the villas in Drezner Street lies nothing more. The built-up zone terminates, as if marked out on a drawing board, and nature takes over from here.

Given the unceasing noise of the highway to Haifa, you admittedly cannot forget where you are, but there are good reasons why the residents of the street use this very pleasant, extensive area for riding their bikes, taking walks, holding children's birthday parties and having picnics. The sandstone typical of the coastal region provides fertile soil for plants and for animals that you can watch here in peace. To see a hare or an endangered sand hedgehog you do need a lot of luck and patience, but when the protected sea onions flower in August and September, or the narcissi and Spanish marigolds in winter, visitors have little treasures literally at their feet.

On the east side of the site, near the highway, are burial caves of the Samaritans dating from the 4th and 5th centuries that give this spot some archaeological interest. They were discovered during road works in the early 1950s and later excavated. There are eight tombs in all. They are in varying states of preservation, and the caves were used for burials by the Samaritan community until the time of the rebellions against the Byzantine Empire. The grave goods – jewellery, glass items, coins and an amulet with an inscription in Samaritan – are on display in the museum of antiquities in Jaffa.

Address Access from the crossroads of Dov Gruner and Yekhi'el Dov Drezner Street, Tel Aviv – Ramat Aviv Gimel | Getting there Bus 6, 13 or 24 to Merkas Schuster/Aba Achimeir | Tip At the western end of Drezner Street is the Rozin Community Center, where many concerts are held as well as weekly leisure activities for people of all ages (www.facebook.com/rozin.center).

# 3__ The Alfred Institute
*A cooperative for art and culture*

A group of thirteen artists got together in 2005 with the idea for something completely new in the Israeli art world. They opened a cooperative gallery where they exhibited their own work and also gave young artists the opportunity to display their works for the first time. Before long the Alfred Gallery had to move to larger premises, and following three further moves it occupied the building at Simtat Shlush 5 in February 2014. Since that time, the concept of a cooperative gallery has been copied several times. But the 'Alfreds' wanted to achieve more.

The Cooperative Institute for Art and Culture, as Alfred is now called, wants to turn a vision into reality. Its founders see themselves as a social institution that is dedicated to bringing about a true encounter between art and interested members of the public. The three-storey building therefore has plenty of space for workshops, talks and seminars in addition to its exhibition rooms on the ground floor. Every week there are events ranging from introductory courses on drawing to literary evenings, art consultations, municipal events and holiday programmes for children. On the upper floors there are also studios, mainly for young artists who are starting out on their careers. Visitors can walk up and look around, which gives the artists an opportunity to present their works to a wider audience while they are still creating them. The large attractive courtyard of the institute is a space for events, but also simply a place to sit and chat. Sometimes outdoor sculptures are on display here. The institute is a wonderfully pleasant place in which to experience art – a world away from the snobbery of many established galleries. It is fitting that this building at the edge of Neve Tzedek was the home of the communist newspaper Kol haAm, the 'voice of the people', in the 1950s.

Address Simtat Shlush 5, Tel Aviv – Neve Tzedek | Getting there Bus 40, 41 to Machon Avni/Eilat | Hours Tue–Thu 5–9pm, Fri 10am–2pm, Sat 11am–3pm | Tip Around the institute you can find a lot of street art, for example directly opposite a large work by Klone, one of the founders of street art in Israel who took the step up to exhibiting in big museums some time ago.

# 4 The American Colony

*A trip to the 19th century*

If you turn into little Auerbach Street from noisy Eilat Street, you might think you have entered a different century. The quiet neighbourhood that lies round the street corner is Tel Aviv's American Colony. In 1866, a group of 157 Christians from Maine in the USA set out for the Holy Land, taking wooden prefabricated houses with them. Most of the colonists gave up quickly and soon returned to Maine. Their houses were sold, and German Templers moved in. The American Colony became a German colony. In the Second World War the government of the British Mandate expelled the Germans. The colony was abandoned, went through a number of changes, and was not finally brought back to life until about 10 years ago. Many of the original houses have unfortunately been demolished, but some have been lovingly restored – for example no. 4 Auerbach Street, a typical example of the colony's building style with a wooden porch and balcony. At no. 10 Auerbach Street, a couple named Holmes opened the Maine Friendship House after giving the wooden building a major restoration. The small museum in the basement tells the story of the American colonists.

Next to it is the Church of Emmanuel, which was consecrated in 1904. Opposite stands the imposing Beit Immanuel, which looks back on a very eventful history: it is the former headquarters of the Templer Society, later a hotel run by the grandfather of Peter Ustinov, and the present-day hostel operated by the Church's Ministry Among Jewish People, an institution that meets severe criticism for its missionary work specifically aimed at Jewish organisations.

If you take a stroll through this district you will find more beautiful houses, some of which have recently been renovated. That the American Colony is still something of a secret for insiders is surely due to the fact that there are no coffee houses in its little streets.

Address Auerbach Street, Bar Hoffman Street, haRabi miBachrach Street, Tel Aviv –
Jaffa North | Getting there Bus 40 or 41 to Machon Avni/Eilat | Hours Museum in
the Maine Friendship House Fri noon–3pm, Sat 2–4pm | Tip Eilat Street is the place
for buying picture frames. Frame shops are lined up here, one next to the other. You can
also find stylish mirrors and small gifts here.

# 5 Art at the Bus Station
*Street art on the seventh floor*

Why Tel Aviv of all places had to have the world's second-biggest bus station is a riddle bequeathed by the urban planners. The city itself only has about 400,000 inhabitants, the Gush Dan metropolitan region 3.4 million. By comparison, in Delhi, where the biggest bus station was constructed, and its surroundings, the population is no less than 16 million. The new central bus station in Tel Aviv has been operating since 1993. Even when it was still being planned in the 1960s it accelerated the decline of the Neve Sha'anan district (see ch. 71).

This concrete monstrosity, which looks fairly harmless from the street, reveals the pitfalls of its construction only when you have entered and are looking for the right bus or some specific destination. There are more than 1,500 shops and stalls here. The 29 escalators and 13 lifts are difficult to find, ensuring that a visit to the bus station is hard work. Shoes, clothing, CDs, accessories for mobile phones, DVDs and all kinds of snack bars, but also institutions such as the Levinsky Clinic for refugees, synagogues, churches, sex shops and a dance club have all found a home here. If you discover the escalators on the seventh floor, you leave all the bustle behind and enter a different world. Up here, at Terminal Dan, buses depart for the Tel Aviv area. It is quiet, clean and not smelly, the ceiling is high, you see the roof and ventilation pipes. And there is art.

The Seventh Floor was the name of an exhibition of street art in June 2013 on the walls of Terminal Dan. The works have remained, and many new ones have been added. You can walk a circuit of this level and marvel at the diversity of the street art, most of it from Israel. Sometimes on a large scale, sometimes meticulously detailed work, the images fit quite naturally into the surroundings. It can only be hoped that this remains as a permanent exhibition.

**Address** Levinsky Street 106, Tel Aviv – Neve Sha'anan | **Getting there** All lines to the central bus station, e.g. 4, 5, 54 and 89 to Tachana Merkasit | **Tip** Artists of the Onya Collective are working at the central bus station on a model project about urban agriculture. You can see it at, for example, the former entrance ramp to Neve Sha'anan Street (see onyacity.com).

# 6 Artik Tivi

*A portion of fruit, not only in summer*

Banana, chocolate, lemon – summer is ice cream time. In Israel, the summer lasts a long time, so there are good reasons to indulge in something cool and sweet almost all year round. If you want to avoid the classic offerings filled with additives and calories that the usual vocal ice cream vendors sell on the beach and in parks, Priz is a fantastic alternative that sells artik tivi (natural ice). Lots of fruit, not much sugar, and water – that's all. No preservatives or colourings. In theory you can make something like this at home, but it is the precise mixture that makes these fruity iced lollipops so delicious.

Priz, a play on words from 'pri' (Hebrew for fruit) and 'freeze', is managed by two brothers, Sharon and Kfir Abu. In a break between jobs, Sharon travelled in South America and looked for a business idea, which he finally found in the form of fruit ices. In Mexico he learned about the production of pure fruit ice, which he then made in Hadera and sold, with little success at first. Large pieces of fruit, as contained in the Mexican original, were not popular in Israel. The breakthrough came only when he made a version in which the fruits are puréed to an even, thick consistency. Priz now sells its wares to companies, the air force and the president.

In addition to the home branch in Netanya, Priz has opened a shop in Tel Aviv. In its first summer, 2012, the outlet was at the centre of real hype, and its new fruit-ice creations were the talk of the whole neighbourhood. Strawberry-banana is the children's favourite, coconut the clear front-runner with adults. But guava, pineapple, lychee, strawberry-kiwi, lemon-mint, passionfruit, banana-date and of course prickly pear are also not to be sniffed at. At eight shekels for a large portion and four shekels for a small one, the ices cost more than their chemical cousins, but it's worth paying the price.

Address Ibn Gvirol Street 158, Tel Aviv – New North | Getting there Bus 25, 26 or 189 to Ibn Gvirol/Pinkas | Hours Sun–Wed 9.30am–11pm, Thu 9.30am–midnight, Fri 9am until 30 minutes before the start of Shabbat, Sat from end of Shabbat until midnight | Tip A wonderful place to eat ice cream is Fruchter Square, diagonally opposite, where the box office for Kastel used to be, which is a small but mighty street café today. On hot days you can cool off in the shade by the newly restored fountain.

# 7 — Artists' Alley

*Through side streets to the New North*

Between busy Pincas Street with the Akirov skyscrapers and their luxury apartments and Yehuda haMaccabi Street, which is highly popular with habitués of coffee houses, lie a few small streets that have kept their original character and still consist entirely of single-storey buildings. South of Yehuda haMaccabi, both Veidat Kattovitz Street and haRav Friedman Street have remained modest. Nevertheless, or perhaps for this very reason, this has become one of the most sought-after and expensive neighbourhoods in the New North, as the district is called.

Building work did not take place here until after 1949, although the basis was established for it in the 1930s. The land had belonged to a German, who was expelled from the country during World War II. It was mainly a district of workers, but also of many artists, and this is still the case today; the dancer Rina Sheinfeld, for example, lives in Friedman Street. In the early days, many artistic people could not afford to live in the city centre. The essence of this whole quarter is best revealed in Birenboim Street, which connects the end of Friedman Street to Veidat Kattovitz Street. The section that is closed to traffic was home to the sculptor Moshe Sternschuss and his wife, the painter Ruth Zarfati, the sculptor Moshe Ziffer, and Arieh Merzer, an artist famous for his copper reliefs. Memorial plaques testify to their work.

Little Birenboim Street was named after the publicist and translator Nathan Birnbaum. And it is no irony of fate that the man who coined the term Zionism, of all people, has been commemorated with such a small street. Shortly after the First Zionist Congress, Birnbaum had a disagreement with Theodor Herzl and turned his back on the movement. This district is seen at its best in July, when the flame trees in Veidat Kattovitz Street rain down their yellow flowers.

בבית זה חי ויצר
האמן
אריה מרזר
1905 - 1966 תרס״ה - תשכ״ו
THE ARTIST
ARIEH MERZER
LIVED & WORKED IN THIS HOUSE

Address Birenboim Street, between Zirelson and Veidat Kattovitz Street, Tel Aviv – New North | Getting there Bus 5, 7 or 25 to Yehuda haMaccabi/Derech Namir | Tip Café Buke at no. 37 Yehuda haMaccabi Street has become the new star on the café strip in the north of the city. Simple, moderately priced vegetarian meals are true organic treats here.

# 8_ The Azrieli Center
*A bird's-eye view of Tel Aviv*

They are almost a landmark of the city: the Azrieli Towers. A circular, a triangular and a rectangular high-rise, together with one of the country's biggest shopping centres, make up the Azrieli Center. Apart from these shapes it is the façades, consisting of thousands of glittering blue windows with white surrounds, that make the Azrieli Center something special. At 187 metres with 49 storeys, the circular tower is the tallest in the ensemble. The triangle is three storeys smaller, and the rectangle, with 'only' 42 storeys, is the smallest of the three. The first two were completed in 1998, then construction of the rectangular tower was put on ice and did not restart until a legal dispute with the city government of Tel Aviv had ended, and was concluded in 2007.

The towers mainly house offices and conference centres, but also a hotel, and on the 49th floor of the round tower there is a viewing deck. The entrance is in the shopping mall, where you can see the three high-rises above you through the glass dome. Its top floor gives access to the lifts that go up to the viewing deck. At 22 NIS for adults and 17 NIS for children the ride up is not cheap, and if you expect a state-of-the-art lift with doors that open quickly, you will be disappointed. The high-class restaurant at the top is of course only open to those who want to dine there. One large room that takes up most of the area of the floor is used for events, and sometimes you have to pick your way between the remains of the most recent occasion.

Ultimately this does not matter, as the fantastic view makes up for everything! On clear days, you can see the whole surrounding country. From the 49th floor you discover a completely new aspect of Tel Aviv. The main roads, the parks, the skyscrapers: from a bird's-eye view, everything has different dimensions and structures that you never noticed before.

**Address** Derech Menachem Begin / Eliezer Kaplan Street, Tel Aviv – Montefiori, +972 (3)6081990-4, www.mitzpe49.co.il | **Getting there** Many buses, e.g. 1, 40, 42, 51, 60 or 63 to Kenyon Azrieli / Derech Begin | **Hours** Vary | **Tip** A futuristic pedestrian bridge links the Azrieli Center to one of the city's central stations, haShalom. From there you have a beautiful view of the illuminated towers by night.

# 9 __ The Banyan Fig
*Playing Tarzan in Azorei Hen*

In the far north of the city, where Tel Aviv peters out in newly built districts, there are few interesting sights. One residential area adjoins the next, and houses are built one onto the other as in a honeycomb, all looking the same. The most exciting thing here is the path to the beach. Here you will find a pretty park on the edge of the Azorei Hen estate. It is known grandiosely as 'gan-ed meyasdey haIr', the 'garden monument for the founders of the city'. This little green space was created by the developer of the residential estate, and as this happened by chance in 1999, the 90th anniversary of the foundation of the city was the inspiration behind the name. The event is commemorated with a nicely designed memorial stone at the corner of the street named after the Yiddish author Uri Zvi Greenberg.

The park has a playground and a fountain in the shape of a Star of David, and is nothing special apart from the lawn itself: lush green grass is not taken for granted in Tel Aviv. The local children use it to play football and other games.

The real gem here is at the edge of the park, close to the street: a banyan fig tree. This variety of the genus Ficus puts out a lot of air roots, especially in moist places – of which Tel Aviv is one. In summer the air humidity is 70 per cent. The roots first extend the circumference of the tree, and over time grow down into the ground, so that it appears to have dozens and dozens of small trunks.

The banyan here is a particularly fine specimen on which the growth of the air roots can be observed easily. It has expanded to many times its original size, as most of the roots are now firmly planted in the soil. However, you can still find a few that hang loose, which leads many visitors to swing on them like Tarzan. Even though this is primarily a game for children, the tree is strong enough to take even grown-up Tarzans.

Address Uri Zvi Greenberg Street, close to the roundabout, Tel Aviv – Zukei Aviv | Getting there Bus 125 to Kdoshei haShoa / Zvi Propes | Tip In the little shopping centre opposite, Gelateria Grinberg sells ice cream just like in Italy – no unusual flavours such as hummus or marshmallow but proper Italian ice cream. Beware! A visit to the gelateria can become a calorie-fest, as they also have cake and sweets.

# 10   The Basel Quarter

*Who still remembers the market?*

The area around Basel Street is one of the city's most popular café districts, and has been for many years. It has shown staying power as a leading hip location with a pleasantly tranquil atmosphere. The streets around Bonei-haIr Square are lined by numerous large and small cafés and bistros, as well as clothes and shoe shops, sushi bars, bakeries and patisseries, stores for baby clothes, ice-cream parlours – everything, in short, that the zfonbonim covet. Yes, Basel is the home of the zfonbonim, as the spoilt residents of northern Tel Aviv are called. A much-loved destination remains Lulu in Elkalai Street, even though its bakery is no longer the best in town. And, of course, in the Basel Quarter you will also find the original home of the Vaniglia ice-cream parlours, which have now spread across the whole country.

Not many of those who now come here to drink their café hafuch can remember what dominated the open space in the middle of the district some 20 years ago. Because the existing markets in the city were far from the residents of the northern districts, the Basel Market was opened in the early 1940s for them. In contrast to the other markets at that time it had a roof, a real novelty. Fruit and vegetables, later poultry and fish too, were on sale here. Next to the market hall lay the main municipal fire station, as well as a representation of Magen David Adom, the Israeli equivalent to the Red Cross.

As the years passed, the market attracted fewer and fewer customers. Putting it under a roof proved to have disadvantages as well as benefits, and a parking area for refuse collection trucks right next to it did nothing to improve the smell of the site.

In the 1980s the decision was taken to tear down the market hall. The fire station moved to the harbour, and the whole area was rebuilt, enabling the cafés to take over.

**Address** Basel Street, between Sokolov and Yehoshua Bin Nun Street, Tel Aviv – Old North | **Getting there** Bus 5 to Dizengoff/Basel, bus 25 to Ibn Gvirol/Pinkas | **Tip** Two side streets further, in haBashan Street, a tiny house stands between numbers 1 and 3. A memorial commemorates Rabbi Israel Sassover, who lived here from 1944 to 1946. This was the cover name of the later prime minister Menachem Begin, who then commanded the militant underground organisation Etzel and lived here anonymously with his family.

# 11__ The Beit Ariela Library

*Browsing in an old concrete bunker*

Big old libraries often have a venerable appearance. This cannot be said of Beit Ariela, Tel Aviv's central library, which comes across more like an ugly duckling. Yet this library is certainly old by Israeli standards. It was founded by the first reading circle in Jaffa in 1886. In 1922, named Shaar Zion (Gate of Zion), it was officially declared to be the municipal library, and had its first home at the corner of Herzl and Ahad haAm. In the early 1960s this building had to make way for construction of the Shalom Meir Tower (see ch. 85). The library was given temporary accommodation until it moved into the new building on Shaul haMelech Boulevard in 1977 and was named after the donor's daughter. There are no spacious halls here. Rather, the concrete colossus gives visitors the feeling that they are entering an outsized bunker. Once you have arrived, however, you will gradually discover a number of treasures, as Beit Ariela holds important specialist departments such as the Rambam library with its rabbinical sources, the Israeli Archive of Modern Dance and an archive of Hebrew writers, which contains some 750 personal bequests.

Yet the most attractive part of the library is the pleasant room for reading the newspapers. Here you can spend some enjoyable hours taking a thorough look at the daily papers, and will encounter a mixed assortment of regular readers who come here to browse without being disturbed by the noise of a café or to have more company than at home. The main daily papers of recent decades are freely available on the shelves, and the archive contains the other issues dating back to the 19th century or to the foundation of the publication in question. And even those who cannot understand Hebrew will find plenty to read, from the *Jerusalem Post* to the *Herald Tribune* and the *International New York Times*.

Address Sderot Shaul haMelech 25, Tel Aviv – New North | **Getting there** Bus 9, 38 or 82 to Beit haMishpat / Sderot Shaul haMelech | **Hours** Newspaper reading room Sun–Thu 10am–7pm, Fri 9am–noon | **Tip** In late afternoon the passage from Beit Ariela and the opera house towards the Dubnov Garden turns into a skateboard arena. The skaters' tricks may be much less ambitious than those in other cities, but it is fun to watch them with the museum and opera house as a backdrop.

# 12__ The Beit Daniel Centre

*The liberal way of observing the Shabbat*

In the 19th century, Reform Judaism emerged in Germany as a result of the Enlightenment and emancipation, and accounted for the majority of the so-called United Congregations before 1933. This movement, later known as liberal, disappeared there as a result of the Holocaust. Emigrants strengthened this movement in the USA, where the first congregations formed as early as the first half of the 19th century. Today the World Union for Progressive Judaism, founded in 1926, has 1.8 million members around the world. In Israel, too, there are a couple of dozen congregations scattered across the country, but Reform Judaism is clearly a minority group here. In the Tel Aviv conurbation there is only one such community: Beit Daniel.

Since 1991 Beit Daniel, headed by Rabbi Meir Azari, has worked for pluralist Judaism with its synagogue, religious education and cultural events. Reform Judaism distinguishes between ethical and ritual laws, with the possibility of adapting the latter to circumstances, and compliance with them left to the individual. Women and men have absolutely equal status, which means that women can be called to the Tora and become rabbis. Reform Judaism also recognises same-sex partnerships.

These principles have made Beit Daniel known and popular far beyond the limited circle of its members, and many secular Israelis like to attend. The religious services are held in a lively manner, and are always accompanied by a lot of singing and guitar music. Especially on holy days such as Yom Kippur, Rosh haShanah and Purim, the centre is full of visitors. As Reform Judaism attaches importance to interreligious dialogue, non-Jews are also welcome at all times. For those who are going to a synagogue for the first time, the best occasion to visit Beit Daniel is the Kabbalat Shabbat on Friday evening, which is open to all.

**Address** Bnei Dan Street 62, Tel Aviv – New North, www.beit-daniel.org.il | **Getting there** Bus 5, 7, 25 or 89 to Yehuda haMaccabi/Derech Namir | **Hours** The website shows times of worship and the programme of cultural events | **Tip** In Jaffa Beit Daniel has a further centre, Mishkenot Ruth Daniel, which alongside its religious services has guest accommodation and runs guided tours of Jaffa.

# 13__Beit haYotzer

*You know where the money is going*

Earning a living as a musician is difficult everywhere. In Israel this is especially true – not only because the market is smaller than in Europe or America, but also because the arts are the first field in which money is saved in times of crisis. Even though it is then more necessary than ever. Musicians outside the mainstream have a particularly hard time. This is where an excellent initiative by Acum, the Israeli association that represents the rights of musicians, writers and publishers, is so valuable: Beit haYotzer ('House of the Creator').

Since 2012 the approximately 8,000 members of Acum have had access to a stage that they can use at no cost in the entertainment district at the port. Acum provides infrastructure such as advertising, sound, lighting, ticket sales and everything else, but charges no fees. All of the income from ticket sales goes to the artists, in contrast to the situation in other clubs, where 50 per cent is often taken by the organiser. This support enables young artists who are setting out on their career to get on stage, and established musicians have an opportunity to present new projects. The programme, consisting of several events daily, is therefore a colourful mix: rock, pop, alternative music, jazz, flamenco and children's concerts at weekends (pictured here: Arik Livnat) – a bit of everything. Beit haYotzer is also a literature venue for readings and workshops.

The plain but high-ceilinged room in a hangar ensures a pleasant atmosphere. When chairs are set out, Beit haYotzer holds about 140 people, so the surroundings are always fairly intimate, and the mood is usually extremely laid-back and friendly. There is a small bar for refreshments. And while audiences listen to the music they can tell themselves with a clear conscience that they have made a good choice by giving direct support to the artists.

**Address** Hangar 22, Namal Tel Aviv, www.bama.acum.org.il (only in Hebrew), acumnamal@gmail.com | **Getting there** Bus 4 or 13 to Dizengoff / Zidon, bus 11 to haYaron / Shaar Zion | **Hours** Almost daily, either at 7pm or 8pm – see website | **Tip** The hangar next door is home to the Zezeze architecture gallery, the only one in the city devoted entirely to architectural projects and the built environment. It exhibits both Israeli and international work (www.zezezegallery.com).

# 14 The Bench at the Marina

*A perfect spot by the sea*

Tel Aviv and the sea are inextricably connected. The city extends almost 15 kilometres along the coast with its beaches and harbours. In contrast to many European cities on the Mediterranean, Tel Aviv has neither idyllic bays nor clear blue water. The sand is fine-grained, which is partly the reason why the water has a muddy, light-brown colour. It happens again and again that a stretch of beach is closed when a municipal sewer is broken, and then the things that flow into the sea make you long for the usual plastic litter that floats there.

If you want a Mediterranean feeling that is a little more romantic, head for the marina. The place buzzes, especially at weekends. Boats go out to sea early in the morning, and some do not return until the late afternoon. The marina has six piers, surrounded by a large harbour wall that acts as a breakwater. The harbour accommodates 320 boats with a length of up to 20 metres. The marina has a café and a restaurant, ships' chandlers selling sailing equipment and also, incidentally, the cleanest public toilets by a long way.

Apart from private yachts, the marina is also the port where sea scouts set out on their tours, and associations such as Etgarim (see ch. 34) hold their activities here. At the end of the entrance area opposite the harbour wall, which has a small lighthouse with green and white stripes at its tip, a bench stands on a concrete base, looking slightly lost. Next to it have been placed two further concrete bases on which there is a steel construction – looking equally lost, and resembling a flower. It remains a mystery whether this is a work of art, as nobody knows anything about it. Nevertheless, this is a wonderful place to sit for a while if you are lucky enough to find the bench unoccupied. Here you can linger and see the boats sailing in and out of port, or watch the sun sink below the horizon.

Address Tel Aviv Marina, at the end of Sderot Ben Gurion, Tel Aviv – Old North |
Getting there Bus 4, 10 or 13 to Ben Yehuda/Arlozorov | Tip In the exclusive Blue
Sky Restaurant on the top floor of the Carlton Hotel, right on the beach in front of the
marina, you can enjoy the view of the sea and the city over a cup of coffee or a long
drink on the roof terrace even if you are not a hotel guest.

# 15 The Benyamini Centre
*Hands-on ceramic art*

On the edge of Kiryat haMelacha (see ch. 56), the Benyamini Centre for contemporary ceramics was set up a few years ago. The small white building is an outsider in the best sense of the word, not only visually, and is more than merely a gallery: it is also a studio, a place devoted to active teaching and learning. It is not restricted to artists, but consciously intends to enter into a dialogue with wider audiences, who are invited to join in with their own hands.

The courses that are held here are addressed to advanced-level ceramic artists as well as to beginners of all age groups who would like to get the feel of working with clay on the potter's wheel. Those who would simply prefer to watch the making of pottery can do so from a gallery on two levels.

The exhibitions change every two months or so. In addition to this, gallery talks, guided tours and other events also take place. A well-stocked library on the subject of ceramic art rounds off the facilities at the Benyamini Centre. Young artists who are just setting out receive support: three guest potters at a time can use a small studio for a year.

The guiding principles behind this institution derive from two ceramic artists, Issachar and Jehudit Benyamini, who ran a small pottery studio in their own house in the north of the city, working and teaching there. In 1990 Issachar was killed in a terrorist attack during a visit to Egypt. His wife Jehudit had the idea of turning their shared home into a centre for art. Her former pupil and friend Marcelle Klein later succeeded in making this wish come true in a different location. The special atmosphere, which guests notice immediately on entering, makes the Benyamini Centre a place where visitors can see and experience the creation of art, and in this way quite simply feel the desire to engage in artistic activity themselves.

**Address** haAmal Street 17, Tel Aviv – Herzl Hill (Givat Herzl) | **Getting there** Bus 3, 19 or 72 to Schocken/Derech kibbutz Galuyot | **Hours** Gallery Mon–Thu 11am–7pm, Fri & Sat 11am–2pm | **Tip** At the corner of Schocken Street is the main building of the daily newspaper *Haaretz*. Amos Schocken's art collection is unfortunately open only to employees, but you can glance inside the lobby, where some paintings are hung – as well as title pages of the latest issue and supplements.

# 16_ The Blue House
*Lea Goldberg's Arnon Street*

'Arnon Street is not the biggest street in Tel Aviv. On the contrary, it is a small street, almost an alley. ... Only small cars drive through it, and just occasionally a truck passes by. And the less traffic in the street, the more children there are.' Many decades have passed since Lea Goldberg started her children's book *My Friends from Arnon Street* with these lines. Not much has changed since then. Arnon Street is still a small, quiet side street without through traffic, where you come across more sleepy cats than pedestrians. There are fewer children now, however, and instead the number of celebrities has grown.

Lea Goldberg, who was born in 1911 in Königsberg, grew up in Kaunas in Lithuania, then studied and gained her doctorate in Berlin and Bonn. In 1935 she emigrated to Palestine and lived at number 15 Arnon Street for 20 years, before moving to Jerusalem, where she taught at the Hebrew University. She was a charismatic author, who never married and lived with her mother. Lea Goldberg wrote prose, poetry and plays, was an excellent translator and was also the author of a number of children's books that have become part of the canon of classic Israeli children's literature.

In the foreword to a new edition of *My Friends from Arnon Street* Goldberg emphasises that many of the things in the book really happened as she described them. She really did live in Arnon Street and there really was a blue house like the one that appears in the story about Uri from the Blue House.

All visitors who come here can see for themselves that this house is still standing today. When you contemplate the blue-painted Bauhaus dwelling at number 9, you cannot help assuming that time has stood still here. The family of the man who built it, Uriel Rosner, still lives there. Rosner chose the colour as a symbol of Jewish labour and the kibbutz.

Address Arnon Street, Tel Aviv – Old North | Getting there Bus 4, 10 or 13 to
Ben Yehuda / Sderot Ben Gurion | Tip At the end of the street a small park with a
playground named after Eran Weichselbaum is a nice place to take a rest. Eran grew
up in Arnon Street and died in 1992 during military exercises.

# 17__ The Bohemian Quarter

*Homes for workers in the International Modern style*

In the 1930s, the idea of the cooperative was applied to urban building, and a series of residential blocks for workers was constructed. They were conceived as small independent estates with grocer's shops and kindergartens; clothes were washed communally on the roof, and the large green area in the courtyard enabled residents to grow vegetables. In Tel Aviv, a total of eight of these Meonot Ovdim were built. One of them was Meonot Hod. Its three connected blocks, forming a U-shape at the crossing of the parallel roads Dov Hoz and Frug Streets with Frishman Street, are known for their central location and an illustrious group of former residents.

Trade unions and the Jewish National Fund acquired the land on which the workers' housing was built based on European models between 1935 and 1945. The architect Arie Sharon, who had been trained at the Bauhaus in Dessau and immigrated to Palestine in 1920, planned the homes in the International Modern style. This small kibbutz at the heart of the city had many famous residents, from politicians and trade unionists to people from the arts world. They included Levi Eshkol, the former prime minister; Mordechai Namir, later mayor of Tel Aviv and minister of labour; the pianist Pnina Salzman; Moshe haLevy, founder of the theatre 'haOhel'; and many others. Hagana, a military organisation before the state of Israel was established, had its headquarter in Meonot Hod in the apartment of Joseph Avidar, one of the founders and commanders of the organisation.

In these streets, more housing blocks were later built, occupied especially by actors at haBima and haOhel. Moshe Feldenkrais, founder of the method of exercise named after him, also lived here. Today many memorial plaques on the buildings of Dov Hoz and Frug serve as reminders of these people and are a good reason to take a stroll around the Bohemian Quarter.

**Address** Intersection of Frishman Street with Dov Hoz and Frug, Tel Aviv – Old North | **Getting there** Bus 5, 22, 39 or 61 to Dizengoff/Beit Lessin or Dizengoff/Frishman | **Tip** For refreshments after a walk through the area, go to Tamara, no. 96 Ben Yehuda Street, right at the corner of Gordon Street, for fantastic frozen yoghurt with fresh fruit, nuts and other toppings, as well as Heidi swings.

# 18__ The Botanical Garden

*Watch the roots grow*

It may not equal the great European gardens, but the Botanical Garden of Tel Aviv University is nevertheless a wonderful island of green that has great charm precisely because it is much less orderly than its European counterparts. It was founded in 1973 and is now a habitat for some 3,800 species of plants. Its primary purpose is teaching and research for the university.

Plants native to Israel and the region are cultivated here, showing the diverse flora of the different climatic regions of Israel, from Mediterranean dwarf scrub typical of the coasts to desert vegetation and wetland plants such as water lilies and papyrus. But the garden also has plants from all around the world, a palm house, succulents and cacti, a tropical house, crop plants and much more. One special field of interest is the preservation of species that are threatened with extinction. Many teaching events that are not directly connected with the university, particularly in the specialised collection of medicinal plants, are also held on the site.

In the warm months of the year, children from the summer camp of Campus Teva get enjoyment from their love of nature in the garden. With a little luck, as a private visitor you can walk on winding paths in relative solitude, in spite of all these activities, forgetting that you are in the middle of a large city. When you encounter a class of school kids, there is only one thing to do: wait for a while on one of the benches in the idyllic surroundings.

One feature of the garden gives it a distinctive status in the world: the growth of roots is investigated in an aeroponic laboratory. For this purpose, a cave-like cellar was built that makes it possible to grow roots in four six-metre-high rooms by providing them with moisture and nutrients, but without soil, thus gaining insights into methods of cultivation and environmental influences.

Address Klausner Street, Tel Aviv University, entrance opposite gate 2 of the university site | Getting there Bus 7 or 25 to Beit haTfuzot / Klausner | Hours Sun – Thu 8am – 4pm, tropical houses 8am – 2.30pm; on the last Friday of the month there is a free tour of the garden at 9am | Tip The 800-metre-long Science Promenade along the Botanical Garden as far as the University train stop reveals stunning views of north-east Tel Aviv and its surroundings. The building of the Porter School of Environmental Studies is one of the world's 'greenest' buildings.

# 19__Boulevard Cafés

*Ben Gurion in a coffee cup*

One of the best-known historical photographs of Tel Aviv shows Rothschild Boulevard only a few years after the city was founded: rows of houses on sand, the Herzliya Hebrew Gymnasium, a high school, in the distance, and not a tree in sight. But there was already a kiosk in the middle of the great 'boulevard'. This mother of all kiosks still exists on Rothschild, although it is now much hipper. Whereas normal kiosks, even in Tel Aviv, sell newspapers, drinks and sweets, on the boulevards (Sderot in Hebrew) they have turned into small boutique cafés that draw hordes of caffeine addicts.

The cafés on Ben Gurion Boulevard are particularly attractive. This kilometre-long avenue, less chic than its big brother Rothschild, leads from the northern end of Rabin Square via Dizengoff Street and Ben Yehuda Street to Atarim Square. And so you can eat and drink your way through the cafés from city hall to the sea.

The starting point is the relatively new Safsal at the corner of Shlomo haMelech, which serves warm food. On the next corner Cafecito, where the customers mainly come from the local neighbourhood, is an institution. From 6 o'clock in the morning until 1 o'clock in the night you can get coffee and sandwiches here at reasonable prices. At the corner of Dizengoff Street stands the newly opened Le CaPhe, a cross between an Italian café-bar and a Vietnamese snack bar, which already has a branch on Ben Zion Boulevard. If you continue past the Tamara juice bar, where wonderful fruit juice in all imaginable combinations is served, you come to the last crossroads on Ben Yehuda Street. Here a dreamy little pale-blue building, Berale, forms the conclusion to the tour at its southern end. At Berale you get only coffee, good coffee, and delicious pastries. Each café has its own rhythm, style and clientele, and there is a place to suit everybody.

**Address** Along Sderot Ben Gurion, Tel Aviv – Old North | **Getting there** Bus 10 to Sderot Ben Gurion/Shlomo haMelech, bus 25 or 26 to Iriat Tel Aviv/Ibn Gvirol | **Hours** One of them is always open, even on the Shabbat | **Tip** At the Sderot Ben Gurion/Adam haCohen intersection in the middle of the boulevard is a memorial to three young women who were killed here in a Palestinian suicide attack in March 1997. The artist Eliezer Weishoff made a stone with three wilted roses in their memory.

# 20  The Bridal Mile

*Weddings start on Dizengoff Street*

Strolling along Dizengoff Street, window-shopping beneath large shady trees on broad pavements, stopping for refreshments in a café and chatting with friends – this used to be so popular that it even led to the creation of its own verb in Hebrew: l'hizdangef. But the glory days of this street ended long ago. In the 1950s and 1960s Dizengoff Street was the centre of bohemian life in Tel Aviv, when people met in the numerous cafés, especially the legendary Kassit.

Named after the first mayor of Tel Aviv, Meir Dizengoff, in his lifetime, the street connects areas of the city centre from Ibn Gvirol to the port in the north. To this day, fashion boutiques and cafés are dominant on what was once a strip for the chic set. A decline began in the 1980s. The opening of the Dizengoff shopping centre in 1977 had a damaging effect, and the remodelling of Dizengoff Square, named after Dizengoff's wife Zina, also detracted greatly from the street's charm (see ch. 29).

Even though Dizengoff has made something of a comeback in recent years, it is no longer the place to come shopping for unusual and original fashion – unless, that is, you want to get married! Towards its north end, around the crossing with Arlozorov Street, on a stretch of some 800 metres, practically every other shop sells bridal fashion. One next to another, they display the latest creations costing tens of thousands of shekels in an attempt to outdo their competitors. For variety, there is a beauty salon or shoe shop that specialises in bridal footwear. Especially on Tuesdays, a popular day for weddings in Israel, you can come to see brides putting on their finery, because this often happens right here, at the shops of the designers, who make the final adjustments themselves. The nervous bridegrooms wait at the door next to decorated cars before the couples drive off for their new lives together.

# 21___The Chanut Theatre

*Alternative art in a showcase*

Aliya Street is in a way the little brother of Allenby Street, of which it is the continuation, and purely a shopping street. In the 1930s the first market hall in the city was built here, and nearby Levinsky Market extends this far. Between shops selling vegetables and eggs, and many selling alcohol, a small and unusual store catches the eye: in the shop window at number 31 you will not find products, but art.

'The shop' is the simple name of the small theatre that occupies this building. Even in its close season it presents small exhibitions in the window, and sometimes live music can be heard too. This ambitious project was initiated by Shachar Marom and Oded Wertsch with the aim of providing a stage for alternative art forms.

Above all else, haChanut is a home for object theatre – which makes it unique in the whole country. This art form, related to puppet theatre, is growing rather hesitantly in Israel. Marom, who plays puppet and object theatre himself, has provided this home for the genre, and the best artists in the field perform here. But haChanut stages much more than this, and is enormously versatile: drama, modern dance, concerts, performances for children, screenings of video art – all of this can be seen in the small converted shop. It is also possible to attend many events in this little treasure-house without being able to understand Hebrew.

As a warm-up act, there is often also a performance in the shop window. Chairs for the audience are then placed on the pavement – to the astonishment of passers-by, who often join the proceedings. After that, the audience members push through the dark curtain to reach the interior of the theatre. It has only 30 seats. A more intimate venue with closer contact to the artists is hardly possible. This is part of the artistic concept and at the same time a statement about an alternative form of cultural activity.

**Address** haAliya Street 31, Tel Aviv – Neve Sha'anan, www.hanut31.co.il (only in Hebrew), hanut.gallery@gmail.com | **Getting there** Bus 3, 19 or 25 to haAliya/Wolfson | **Tip** At the north end of Aliya Street is Kikar haMoshavot, where several main roads meet. In the 1930s a roundabout with a fountain and lawn was laid out, but later removed. Today a column displaying historical photos serves as a reminder of how the street scene once looked.

# 22 Charles Clore Park
*Where young and old cool off*

Water is precious in Israel. There are only a few places in Tel Aviv where children, both young and old, can play in water. One of them is in Charles Clore Park, the continuation of the beach promenade beyond the dolphinarium. The mile-long park was laid out in the 1970s on the remains of Manshiye, an Arab quarter that once belonged to Jaffa. After the War of Independence, the city authorities decided to demolish the decaying quarter, which had been partly abandoned. The rubble from the demolition was used to landscape the hills in the new park.

The park has only a light covering of trees, and orientation is therefore very easy. The large expanses of lawn are used by both Jewish and Arab residents of the city as places to relax or have a picnic. On summer evenings, a thick cloud of barbecue smoke hangs in the air here. At its south end lies the Etzel Museum. A statue by Ilana Gur, *Woman Against the Wind*, leans into the sea breeze here. The coastal strip in the park, called Alma Beach, is fairly small but pleasantly quiet with a nice family atmosphere.

In 2009, the restoration of Charles Clore Park was completed. The equipment for children is especially good. In this way, an old tradition has been continued, as there was always a wonderful playground in the park. Now it also has water for splashing around, and of course this is the great attraction in summer. On a circular area, a couple of dozen jets spout water from the ground at varying intervals of time, and younger children are not the only ones who just love it. In the evening, groups of young people often take the place of the children, and at night the fountain jets have revived many an adult who has been out on the town and been drinking anything but water. In contrast to the scene by the harbour, where there is an identical fountain, Charles Clore Park is a much quieter spot.

Address Charles Clore Park, Tel Aviv – Neve Tzedek; the fountain is not far from the petrol station | Getting there Bus 10, 11, 18 or 37 to Prof. Kaufmann/Shenkar | Hours Accessible 24 hours | Tip Mantaray, one of the city's best fish restaurants right on Alma Beach, where you can trail your toes through the sand, has now opened a kiosk. You can order a few light dishes there and wash the meal down with a cocktail.

# 23 __ Chavshush

*Spice paradise at Levinsky Market*

There is no shortage of good spices on sale at the market. However, if you are looking for the very best quality and a wide selection at the same time, the place to go is Chavshush. This old-established shop is situated in a side street and easy to overlook, as the only pointer to its existence is a small, inconspicuous sign above a green door that resembles a shipping container. When you walk inside and make your way along the narrow passage between crates and sacks, you are enveloped by strong aromas: turmeric, aniseed, cardamom, cinnamon, nutmeg and other smells fill the air. It is not only the sense of smell that gets stimulated – there is also a feast of colour for the eye, and items to admire that you may well never have seen before. Even avowed fans of pulses will be astonished at all the varieties of lentils, beans and peas before them.

In 1931, the Chavshush family came to Palestine from Yemen and opened their first stall on the Carmel Market. A few years later they moved to Jaffa, near the harbour. Their shop and storehouse were attacked and burned down in 1947 in the troubles leading to the independence of Israel, and the family then opened a new shop on the present site. Arieh Chavshush, who started to work in the shop with his father when he was 20 years old, was born in the house next door in 1947. Today he runs the business with his sons.

Chavshush supplies restaurants and other businesses, but also and especially looks after his 'small customers'. He has a friendly but not pushy manner, a combination not often found at the market, when giving advice about what kind of hummus to buy or which of his own spice mixtures work best with which dishes. He also sells a range of excellent dried fruit, from figs and raisins to apricots and sought-after madjoul dates, as well as stocking all kinds of nuts and various sorts of tea.

Address haChalutzim 18, Tel Aviv – Florentin | Getting there Bus 3, 19 or 25 to
haAliya / Matalon | Hours Sun – Fri 7.30am – 1pm | Tip On the corner of haChalutzim
and Levinsky Street is Boutique Naknik (sausage boutique), a delicatessen with excellent
speciality sausages where you can also buy a freshly made and well-filled sandwich.

# 24 — Chen Boulevard

*On the trail of fruit bats*

Chen Boulevard is one of the city's more modest avenues. In contrast to its big brother Rothschild Boulevard, of which it is the continuation, it can boast no spectacular Bauhaus architecture or hip cafés. Taking its name from an acronym of the given names of the Hebrew poet Chaim Nachman Bialik, Chen also means 'grace'. And that fits this quiet street with its wonderful trees very well.

The Chinese fig trees that dominate the scene produce air roots that wind around the trunk to form an interesting structure that strollers can admire while walking in the middle of the boulevard. This species of tree was planted in Tel Aviv as long ago as the 1920s. It is beautifully green and nicely tall, thus lending a stately appearance to the street. Fig trees also provide a lot of shade, and indeed Chen Boulevard is always a pleasant place, even at the height of summer.

The trees have one big disadvantage, however: their fruit presents the city with a challenge. Three or four times a year the fruits fall to the ground like big marbles and cover it completely, causing accidents and blocking up the drains. Some 20,000 trees make a mess of the city by dropping their fruit. It was not planned to be like this, because a decisive element was missing when the fig trees were first introduced: a kind of tiny wasp, only one millimetre in size, which lives in symbiosis with the trees and ensures that they are fertilised to yield fruit. In the 1970s this little wasp then somehow made its way to Israel and found a veritable unspoiled paradise there. This was a welcome development for the large groups of bats that inhabit the city. They are Egyptian fruit bats, which are exclusively vegetarian. Whenever the fruit of the Chinese fig is ripening again, when darkness falls on Chen Boulevard you can watch a fantastic spectacle of flying bats.

**Address** Sderot Chen, Tel Aviv – Old North; the finest fig trees are between Netsach Israel and Frishman | **Getting there** Bus 18, 25, 38 or 82 to Kikar Rabin/Malkei Israel | **Tip** At the very start of the boulevard is a memorial to the signing of an agreement in the house at no. 1 Sderot Chen on 13 May, 1948 by representatives of the Arab population of Jaffa, in which they handed over the city to Hagana, the leading military force in the country. On the following day, David Ben Gurion declared the founding of the state of Israel.

# 25 The Communal Garden

*A green oasis in Florentin*

The district of Florentin in the south of the city has already been through the process of gentrification. Between small buildings that are still the premises of manual workers, car washes and shops, some of them half decayed and covered in graffiti, rise stylish multi-storey new buildings that contrast jarringly with their surroundings. Nevertheless, Florentin has kept much of its original character, which you can sense best if you take a walk through the little side streets. In one of them, HaRabi MiBachrach Street, you will discover a small oasis amidst the concrete and parked cars: the neighbourhood garden of Florentin.

By planting vegetables, fruit and spices here, the local residents have communally created a little green miracle that makes reality of the dream of a sustainable lifestyle in the city. Beans and mangos, lettuce and rosemary grow here all over the site, encircled by graffiti. Altogether there are almost 40 such neighbourhood gardens scattered across Tel Aviv today, and their numbers are growing. The city government actively supports residents' initiatives and helps in the search for suitable places. The gardens are tended according to the principles of ecological cultivation, i.e. without chemical insecticides and with the gardeners' own compost as fertiliser. The conscious aim of the gardens is to reinforce the local sense of belonging and to connect residents to their district, counteracting the anonymity of the city.

The communal garden in Florentin, founded in 2005, was the first, which is no coincidence. This district has attracted young, alternative-minded, creative people and artists for some time now. Local residents go to the communal garden every Shabbat in the afternoon to sow, dig, remove weeds and eat together. For the rest of the week the garden is open to all, but only those who join in the work are supposed to harvest the fruits.

Address HaRabi MiBachrach Street 12, Tel Aviv – Florentin | Getting there Bus 40,
41 or 240 to Eilat/Elifelet, in the opposite direction to Avni Institute/Eilat | Tip
Right next door is a small shop that calls itself the matkot centre. Here you can get
everything for matkot, a popular beach game played with wooden bats and rubber
balls – in all sizes and colours, and the best quality. The owner speaks no English, but
communication is possible, including hints for beginners.

# 26__The Conservatory

*From new immigrants to the piano, solfège and jazz*

The site in the Old North of the city that is today occupied by the Israel Conservatory of Music has been used for several different purposes. The first building here was the Beit haOlim (House of Immigrants), as the previous Beit haOlim in Aliya Street was hopelessly overcrowded. In those days, the place was closer to the new port, which had been built as a result of Arab unrest that shook the country in 1936, but it was still well off the beaten track and was connected to the city centre by only a single bus route. Here the Keren haYesod movement constructed three buildings in a U-shape and a large communal indoor area. The complex opened in March 1938 and could accommodate 200 new immigrants.

This situation was not to last long. After the Italian air raids on Tel Aviv in 1940 (see ch. 62), an additional hospital was needed to care for the injured. The House of Immigrants was converted, and in 1953 became the Yarkon Hospital, which was then merged with the Tel haShomer Hospital. The building was later used by soldiers and known as Beit haHayal. The Conservatory of Music was not opened until 1983, and thus gained a suitable home some 40 years after its foundation.

Today, about 600 music pupils of all ages study here, receiving a thorough classical education as well as early music training and lessons in singing and jazz. It is well worth checking out the events listings, especially at the beginning and end of the school year, when the students give free concerts that are designed to appeal to the whole family. The original building has now been demolished and replaced. In the new building, a pleasant and inviting outdoor area has been created at the entrance. People like to take a seat on the benches, around the little ecological pool or on the lawn to listen to the music that wafts over from the open windows of the Conservatory.

Address Louis Marshall Street 25, Tel Aviv – New North, www.icm.org.il, secretariat +972 (3)5460524 | **Getting there** Bus 24 or 25 to Yehuda haMaccabi / Ironi Jud Alef, bus 5 or 11 to Pinkas / De Haas | **Tip** On Kikar Milano, the start of Yehuda haMaccabi Street, is one of the most popular cafés in the area, Zorik. It is always full – at weekends you queue to get in – and is sustained mainly by its reputation as a place where hip and beautiful people meet.

# 27 — The Cymbalista Synagogue

*A striking synagogue on the university campus*

Above the Faculty of Humanities, right in the middle of the university campus, lies an architectural gem. Here the Cymbalista Synagogue, which has adorned the campus since 1998, rises like a little fortress. It is marked by the unmistakable style of its architect, Mario Botta, who comes from the Ticino area of Switzerland. The building takes its character from being restricted to simple geometrical shapes. In commissioning Botta, the Swiss donor, Norbert Cymbalista, was turning to an architect who had never before entered a Jewish place of worship. The result is considered today to be one of the most important contemporary synagogue buildings in the world.

It consists of two almost identical square spaces that open up at the top into cylinders. One of them serves as the synagogue, the other as the beit midrash (house of teaching) and assembly room. A small room for studies and a permanent exhibition of Jewish ceremonial art are accommodated in the auxiliary rooms. This division of space justifies the location of the synagogue, not only on the campus, a place of learning, but also in Tel Aviv, a place of diversity: whereas worship in the synagogue takes place according to orthodox rites, the other space is also used for holding conservative and reformed services. For this purpose, there is a mobile torah shrine that can be brought in as needed. Services are held three times daily. Numerous events on a wide variety of subjects, usually about the interface between religion and secularism or about Israeli history and Jewish identity, are open to the general public.

With this warm building, flooded with light despite its lack of windows, Mario Botta made the donor's vision a reality. The Cymbalista Synagogue stands for the diversity of Judaism and its unity, as well as for the significance of history and tradition for modern Jewish identity.

Address University of Tel Aviv campus, entrance through the main gate, then straight up to the synagogue, en-heritage.tau.ac.il, heritage@post.tau.ac.il | Getting there Bus 7 or 25 to haUniversita / Chaim Levanon | Hours These vary according to the season; please refer to the website | Tip Opposite the synagogue is Beit Hatfutsot (Diaspora House), dedicated to Jewish communities in the diaspora. In addition to the exhibition, which is to be renewed in 2018, the museum always puts on several changing shows at the same time (www.bh.org.il).

# 28 Danziger's Serpentine

*A slightly crumbling masterpiece in Yarkon Park*

In the eastern part of Yarkon Park, behind the lake, adventure playground and rock garden, a white, slightly weathered concrete structure stands alone with nothing around it. There is no indication that this is a landscape sculpture by one of the leading Israeli sculptors, who influenced generations of artists in the country. The *Serpentine* is a work by Yitzhak Danziger.

Danziger was born in 1916 in Berlin and came to Palestine in 1923 with his parents. He had his artistic training in London. His first major work was a sculpture of the biblical figure Nimrod (1939), which aroused great controversy. Later he increasingly turned to work on the theme of the interrelationship between humans and nature. For this purpose, he also studied landscape architecture. Danziger was killed in a car accident in 1977. Two years previously he had created the sculpture entitled *Serpentine*. It was commissioned by the city of Tel Aviv for the park, which was opened in 1973. The work rises to a height of 3.70 metres above the grass, as if it had been folded, and its curves reflect the surrounding park landscape. When it was unveiled, the hills of the park were the only things rising above the flat ground. Today they are surrounded by high-rise buildings, and the flumes of the nearby water park are also visible. The varying heights of the walls of the sculpture produce a play of light and shade that constantly changes according to the position of the sun. The white concrete, contrasting with the green grass, can be seen from a distance.

It is a pity that the work looks a little bit shabby today. In various places graffiti has been scrawled on it and not painted over properly, the concrete is crumbling and cracked, and litter often lies in its coils. Nevertheless, *Serpentine* is a place that invites visitors to the park to linger, play and hide.

Address Yarkon Park, east end between car park and Meimadion | Getting there
Bus 12, 22, 40 or 89 to Ganei Yehoshua Sderot Rokach | Hours Accessible 24 hours |
Tip In this part of the park, specially laid-out gardens such as the Tropical Garden
are worth a visit.

# 29 — Dizengoff Square

*Down to earth again*

In the so-called Geddes Plan, the first blueprint for building the city, conceived in the late 1920s by the Scottish urban planner Sir Patrick Geddes, Dizengoff Square was already laid out as a big roundabout for traffic with an open space. It was named after Zina Dizengoff, the wife of Tel Aviv's first mayor, Meir Dizengoff. She died in 1930 at the age of 58. The design of the square is the work of the architect Genia Awerbuch, who won the competition to carry out this task in 1934 with her proposal for complementary, uniformly designed house façades in the International Modern style. All of the buildings around the square were constructed according to Awerbuch's designs.

The square, inaugurated in 1938, quickly became the vibrant focal point of the city, with cafés and cinemas in the surrounding buildings, but in the 1960s and 1970s its popularity declined, above all as a result of the traffic. The mayor in those years, Shlomo Lahat, supported a solution to the problem that was implemented in 1978. A pedestrian level was created above the level of the original square so that the traffic could flow unhindered beneath. The fountain that had previously stood in the middle of the square was replaced a few years later by a kinetic work called *Water and Fire* by Yaakov Agam that is now one of the best-known attractions in Tel Aviv.

This project nevertheless met with a critical reception. The re-modelled square had lost the original charm of a public open space. In the context of the celebrations for the 100th anniversary of the city, the idea was mooted that Dizengoff Square should be restored to its original appearance. Construction work began in December 2016 to tear down the pedestrian level. The fountain by Yaakov Agam will remain part of the newly designed Dizengoff Square, a fact that somewhat dampens the enthusiasm of many citizens for the restoration.

Address Dizengoff Square, Tel Aviv – Old North | Getting there Bus 5, 39, 61, 66 or 72 to Kikar Dizengoff | Tip The popular antiques and second-hand market that used to be held on Dizengoff Square every Tuesday from 11am to 10pm and every Friday from 7am to 4pm has moved to Givon Street near the Cinematheque.

# 30 Drummers' Beach

*A rhythmic start to the weekend*

Ushering in the weekend on a Friday afternoon: anyone who likes things to be really 'shanti' has to go down to Drummers' Beach. Dozens of people assemble here each week to beat drums together by the north wall of the dolphinarium. In winter an intimate little group gets together in the sunshine, and in summer it becomes a big beach party, with people dancing right down to the water. Most of the drummers are men, who display varying degrees of virtuosity.

As far as the dancers are concerned, the majority are women. Many of them show their skills at belly dancing. Sometimes other musical instruments join in, perhaps a flute, guitar or didgeridoo. Occasionally there is juggling, capoeira dance, and in summer after night falls a performance by fire-eaters.

It is fascinating to see how completely different kinds of people congregate here: young and old, alternative and seemingly strait-laced. What they all have in common is a passion for drumming and the rhythm. These meetings of drumming enthusiasts have been taking place for 20 years already. Here Tel Aviv shows its essence: everyone can look the way they want, and do what they want to do. Life is a party, and you don't think about tomorrow if war and terrorism could destroy everything.

The dolphinarium with its faded charm is a fitting backdrop for this. The wall behind the drummers is covered with graffiti, the concrete is crumbling, and the smells left over from the previous night are not always fragrant ones. It is a long time since any dolphins were kept here. Since the mid-1980s the site has been used for holding events and for club nights. On 1 June, 2001 one of the worst acts of terrorism in Israel took place here when a Palestinian suicide bomber took the lives of 21 young Israelis in front of a discotheque. A plaque on the spot commemorates the victims of the attack.

Address Rezif Herbert Samuel, north of Charles Clore Park, Tel Aviv – Neve Tzedek |
Getting there Bus 3, 16, 31, 63 or 66 to Hananiya / haYarkon | Tip The section of beach
immediately to the north is called Banana Beach after its beach bar. Here, too, the mood
is extremely relaxed, and this part of the beach is also popular with young families.

# 31 The Dummy Tree

*If you don't like the dummy fairy*

This idea is not new, especially in child-friendly Scandinavia. As long ago as the 1920s the first dummy tree existed on the Danish island of Thurø. The intention was to help children say farewell to their dummies, which are damaging to the jaw, by means of a little ritual carried out in harmony with nature: they hang their dummies, called 'motzetz' in Hebrew, on a tree. In some European countries, there are publicly accessible dummy trees, and a few years ago the idea took hold in Israel. Kfar Saba has one, and so does Givatayim. And now there is a dummy tree in Tel Aviv too, in Dubnov Park.

Initially the company that operates Yarkon Park tried to establish a dummy tree in the rear part of the park. This seems to have been too far away for most parents. No more than three or four forlorn-looking dummies dangle from the newly planted tree. It is a completely different case with the one at the edge of Dubnov Park, where parents have simply set up a dummy tree themselves. Now dozens of them in all shapes and colours hang from it, and their numbers are growing all the time.

If you really do want to get rid of a dummy there, you'd be well advised to prepare the ground very carefully. The child has to be accustomed to getting the dummy only at certain times. Before paying a visit, you should tell them about it and encourage them in the belief that they are already big, and say you believe that, like all bigger children, they can leave their dummies on this tree.

You can turn the day into a celebration, invite family and friends and organise a picnic – Dubnov Park gives you every opportunity to do this. And when you go home again without the dummy, then you have to be firm. That applies more to the parents than to the child. And as for the dummy, you can come back and visit it, combining this with an afternoon in the big playground.

**Address** Dubnov Park, opposite no. 25 Dubnov Street, Tel Aviv – New North | Getting there Bus 18 or 25 to Kikar Rabin / Malkei Israel, bus 89 to Kikar Rabin / Ibn Gvirol | Tip The Israeli Opera, located above the park, stages regular afternoon performances for children aged 3 to 8. The programme includes *Hansel and Gretel*, *The Magic Flute* and *Figaro* (www.israel-opera.co.il).

# 32 The Eden Cinema

*Where Shirley Temple once danced*

On a visit to Egypt Meir Dizengoff, Tel Aviv's first mayor, saw something that he wanted in his own newly founded city. Something that was indispensable in a proper city: a cinema. It did not take long to find two people to run it. They were Moshe Abarbanel and Mordechai Weisser, who expressed their willingness to invest following assurances that they could have a 15-year exclusive contract. In 1913 they bought land in Lilienblum Street and commissioned a German architect to design an up-to-date building. They bought the projector in Alexandria and ordered seating from Vienna. On 22 August, 1914 everything was ready. The Eden Cinema was inaugurated and screened its first film, a box-office hit called *The Last Days of Pompeii*.

Initial reservations in the neighbourhood, for example about the petrol that was needed for the generator that powered the projector, and also concerns about possible lapses in morals at a place of entertainment, were soon dispelled. The Eden was a success. At first it showed silent films, accompanied by music from an orchestra. In the early years the auditorium was also used as a theatre and concert hall. After World World War I, daily film screenings were held, and the 'summer Eden' was installed in the backyard.

In addition to movies with stars such as Shirley Temple and Charlie Chaplin, the Eden also showed Jewish productions, for example *Dybbuk*. Screenings also took place in Yiddish and Russian, and the advertising was in three languages. After 1948, when many Jews from Arab countries settled in the south of the city, the Eden changed its programme to meet their needs and showed Turkish, Persian and Indian films. The Eden's glory days were already long past by that time, and the cinema closed in 1974. After standing empty for decades, the building is now being converted into a luxury boutique hotel.

**Address** Lilienblum Street 2, Tel Aviv – City Centre | **Getting there** Bus 40 or 41 to Derech Jaffo / Herzl, then a short walk along Pines Street | **Tip** No. 5 Lilienblum Street is home to the Kol Yehuda Synagogue, built in 1938 by the architect Yehuda Magidovich for the Jewish community from Aden in Yemen. Today the Aden Heritage Center presents an exhibition there on the life and culture of Yemeni Jews in Aden and Tel Aviv. Admission is free.

# 33__The Engel Building
*The first building on stilts*

Among all the splendid renovated architectural gems on Rothschild Boulevard there is an ugly duckling, behind whose decaying façade lies what was once a constructional innovation in Tel Aviv: the Engel Building (Beit Engel), number 84, was the first in the city to have pilotis, an open construction with supporting pillars on the ground floor, designed to allow cool air to flow underneath. It was built in 1933 to designs by the architect Zeev Rechter, whose style was strongly influenced by the great French architect Le Corbusier.

The specific model for Beit Engel was Le Corbusier's Villa Savoye in Poissy-sur-Seine, with its pilotis. Apart from its innovative, highly modern method of construction, the building, which Rechter planned for the businessman Yaakov Engel, is a classical Bauhaus structure with clear lines and balconies. The architect himself ran his practice in Tel Aviv until the 1950s.

Rechter had to engage with the city authorities in a lengthy controversy about the designs, as the supporting pillars were not favourably received at first – which is astonishing when you consider that today they are part of the usual urban scene. This mode of construction remained the typical style until well into the 1980s. Regrettably, the original concept was not adhered to. The idea was that there would be a green area beneath each building, thus making it possible to extend public space and provide better circulation of air. Instead of this, today you find only meagre little gardens, if any at all, in the space created by putting the building on stilts. Usually these surfaces are used for parking cars, which is not surprising given that Tel Aviv is bursting at the seams with traffic.

Beit Engel waited a long time to be renovated. The pilotis are only partly visible now, as an additional wall was built, adorned by graffiti, that hides the architectural masterpiece.

**Address** Beit Engel, Sderot Boulevard 84, Tel Aviv – City Centre | **Getting there**
Bus 5 to Rothschild / Maze, bus 70 or 142 to Rothschild / Balfour | **Tip** The street café
called 'R' in the middle of the boulevard, on the corner right in front of Beit Engel, has
delicious sandwiches and a lot of tables from which you can enjoy the scene on
Rothschild Boulevard.

# 34__The Etgarim Centre

*An architectural jewel for a good cause*

It's a real eye-catcher: three flat white buildings, asymmetrical, facing each other, with a sunshade fastened above them. In September 2013, the new centre of the non-profit association Etgarim was unveiled on Raoul Wallenberg Street in the district of Ramat haHayal in the eastern part of Yarkon Park. Etgarim ('challenges') works to give physical and spiritual assistance to people with handicaps by means of diverse kinds of sporting activities. Founded in 1995 by a group of people with handicaps, including many who had been wounded in war, and experts on rehabilitation, it now helps about 5,000 children and young people and 1,000 adults in a variety of projects all over the country.

Etgarim wants to get away from describing people with handicaps as 'people with special needs', and prefers to support them as 'special people', helping them to meet challenges. Extreme sports are a means to this end: with assistance from Etgarim, blind people take part in triathlon events and people with leg amputations participate in bike races. The new centre in Beit Shneur Park is a starting point for bicycle rides in Yarkon Park, organised as tandem tours. For example, blind children can ride bikes through the park with a volunteer.

The centre bears the name of Shneur Chasin, who was killed at the age of 43 while training on his bike in an accident with a driver who fled the scene. The family made a donation towards construction of the building, which was designed by the Yoav Messer architects' office. The three structures are used as an office, a space for events and for storing bikes. The idea of openness in the architecture is evident not only in the completely transparent façades, which have glass fronts on both sides and are covered only by silver sun blinds; there is no separation of the buildings from the park, no fence, no obstacle to encounters.

**Address** Raoul Wallenberg Street, near the crossroads with Mishmar haYarden Street,
Tel Aviv – Yarkon Park / Ramat haHayal | **Getting there** Bus 12, 52 or 189, Raoul
Wallenberg / Mishmar haYarden | **Tip** At the crossing of Raoul Wallenberg and haBarzel,
a sculpture by the Hungarian artist Imre Varga commemorates the eponymous Raoul
Wallenberg, a Swedish diplomat who saved tens of thousands of Hungarian Jews from
deportation to Auschwitz.

# 35__The Former Station

*On the organic track*

Since 2010, what used to be the train station in Jaffa has become a place for strolling and people-watching. For decades it was abandoned and, although it is easy to find on the way from Neve Tzedek to Jaffa, forgotten.

The railway to Jerusalem went into operation in 1892. Theodor Herzl used the train during his journey to Palestine in October 1898: 'It was an ordeal in the cramped, crowded, scorching-hot coupé', he noted in his diary. Nevertheless, the four-hour route to Jerusalem was heavily used by travellers, as it superseded an extremely arduous day-long journey in a coach. The Wieland family, part of the Templer community, took advantage of their closeness to the station and built both their own home and a factory for cement and other construction materials next to the station. Another red building, which has survived to this day, belonged to the Arab Manshiye neighbourhood. All of these different buildings in their own styles have now been beautifully restored. In two historic railway carriages with a multimedia show, visitors can gain an impression of the rail traffic, which was suspended in 1948 during the War of Independence, and later resumed with a new terminus. Apart from this, Tachana ('station') is mainly occupied by expensive designer shops and restaurants, and some art is also on display. The site is truly pleasant on Fridays, when the atmosphere of exclusivity is relieved a little by the weekly organic market. Vegetables and fruit from organic farms, oil, bread, spices, fruit juices, halva, pulses and olives are on sale. You can also have a massage or try out a yoga course. As well as this there are many stands selling snacks. 'Healthy' is the motto here, and in fact that does fit in well with the chic and trendy feel of the place, because in Tel Aviv a healthy lifestyle and organic food are definitely hip.

Address haTahana, Professor Yehezkel Kaufmann Street, at the crossroads with haMered Street, Tel Aviv – Neve Tzedek haTahana | **Getting there** Bus 11, 18 or 37 to Professor Kaufmann / Goldmann, bus 10 to haEtzel / Goldmann | **Hours** Market every Fri 9am – 3pm | **Tip** Next to Tachana is the army museum, which looks at the history of Israel from an unaccustomed perspective, presenting the development of the Israeli army, Zahal (Zwa Hagana leIsrael, army for the defence of Israel) in almost 20 stages. In the outdoor zone all kinds of vehicles are on display, from tanks to rocket launchers and bridging vehicles.

# 36 Gan haHashmal

*What does cheese made from cashews taste like?*

One of the newer trendy quarters of the city is just a few paces away from Allenby Street, in the side streets around the little green patch known as Gan haHashmal. At number 16 Hashmal ('electricity') Street, the city's first power plant went into operation in 1923, generating electricity from a diesel engine imported from Germany.

The little park was very popular among residents of the neighbourhood, both for relaxing during the day and also at night – then, thanks to its dense planting with trees, it was known as Ginat haNeshikot ('garden of kisses'). This romantic aspect was soon over, and as the years passed, the district went downhill. Gan haHashmal became a synonym for underage male prostitution.

In 2003, the city government decided to restore the park, and this resulted in an improvement in fortunes for the whole quarter. In time, more and more young designers set up here, as the rents were lower than elsewhere. Imaginative fashion, shoes and jewellery have now found a home here alongside a lot of new cafés and bars. Especially near the corner of Levontin Street and Barzilai Street there is one café next to another with small but carefully honed menus. A great variety is on offer here, from gourmet hamburgers to creative cakes.

Among the first who ventured into the district were three musicians who opened Levontin 7, at that very address, in 2006. With its daily live music it has long been an institution for all musicians of the alternative scene. The ground floor, separated from the performing space in the basement, has a very popular bar, where you can order one of the best pizzas in the city from haHatul haYarok next door. The dough is thin and crispy, and is covered with wonderful vegan ingredients such as artichokes, mushrooms and sweet potatoes. The cheese is made from cashew nuts, an innovation for the vegan market.

**Address** Levontin / Barzilai / haHashmal Street, Tel Aviv – City Centre | Getting there
Bus 5, 25, 70 or 142 to Allenby / Yehuda haLevy, bus 3, 19 or 72 to Allenby / Derech
Begin | Tip Kuli Alma, a little off the beaten track at no. 10 Mikveh Israel Street, has a
good mix of nightlife with DJs changing daily, good cocktails and presentations of art,
from street art to video works. The bar belongs to a cooperative of Tel Aviv DJs and
artists (www.kulialma.com).

# 37___Gordon Pool

*The city's cleanest sea water*

Swimming pools are a rarity in Tel Aviv. This is partly because water is precious and relatively expensive in the Middle East, but also and especially because the city has enough beaches. Nevertheless, many go swimming in a pool, either as a sport or because they are not lovers of beach life. For all such people, a good place to go is the Gordon Pool – a long-established swimming bath just a few paces north of the beach of the same name.

Built in 1956 by Werner Joseph Wittkower, an architect from Berlin who also drew up the masterplan for the campus of Tel Aviv University and designed several hotels along the coast, the Gordon Pool is extremely popular, especially in summer. Its water – and this is the distinguishing feature of the Gordon Pool – is mineral-rich sea water, taken from a depth of 150 metres by three pumps and heated to a temperature of 24 degrees Celsius. In summer this represents a pleasant cooling-off, though in winter it is only really suitable for really keen sports swimmers. The pool used to be open 364 days a year, and closed only for Yom Kippur. Regular swimmers, most of them from an older age group, often arrived before sunrise to get in their first lengths of the 50-metre pool.

But that was in the best years. The swimming pool aged, and in the end only opened during the summer months. Its private owner, a man who lived in the USA, kept it going, however. After his death, his son made an agreement with the city authorities, who wanted to close the pool altogether. Stubborn protests by regular customers eventually brought about a change of mind, and in 2009, following a three-year phase of reconstruction, the renovated pool opened once again.

It is still emptied completely and pumped full again every day. Especially in summer, people queue up to enjoy clean, cooling water that is free from sand and jellyfish.

Address Eliezer Peri Street 14, Tel Aviv – Yafo | **Getting there** Bus 4, 10 or 13 to Ben Yehuda / Arlozorov | **Hours** Sun 1.30 – 9pm, Mon – Thu 6am – 9pm, Fri 6am – 7pm, Sat 7am – 6pm | **Tip** Café Landwer, right by the entrance to the pool, is one of the nicest in this chain, where you can pass some time on one of the comfortable sofas by the waterside with a view of the marina.

# 38__The Green House

*Past glory in Jaffa*

In Yefet Street, the three-kilometre-long main street of Jaffa, which passes through the Ayami district as far as the city boundary and is lined with shops, there is an architectural survival from the old golden days of Arab Jaffa. It is called the Green House on account of its façade, which is green today with a slight touch of turquoise. This imposing building stands on the corner of Yefet Street and Shivtei Israel Street on raised ground, and used to be visible from far away. Today it has been hemmed in by other buildings, and you can only see the upper storeys, even if you stretch and crane your neck.

The house was constructed in 1934 for the family of Sheikh Ali, a plantation owner and cloth merchant from Jaffa whose father had been mayor of the city for some time. It is a particularly fine example of the architectural style loved by rich Arab families. Its eclectic appearance combines traditional Islamic elements with Art Deco. The covered balconies are supported by columns, symmetrical windows adorn the various wings of the house, and the decoration of the walls corresponds to the balustrade of the top storey. If you take a stroll through Ayami, where most of the streets are much narrower and smaller than Yefet Street, you will spot more buildings of a similar kind. After 1948 Ayami increasingly became a problem area, a theme that was treated in the Oscar-nominated film of the same name in 2009. In recent years, a process of gentrification has set in as a result of several luxurious real-estate developments.

The Green House was used by the army after the War of Independence, first by the intelligence department and later by a military court, which still occupies the building.

Today, it is decaying somewhat. The plaster is peeling and the window shutters are no longer handsome, but it is possible to imagine its former splendour.

**Address** Yefet Street 91, Tel Aviv – Jaffa / Ayami | **Getting there** Bus 10 or 41 to Yefet /
Mendès-France | **Tip** Go a little further along to no. 138 Yefet Street to find one of the
city's legendary ice-cream parlours, Glida Andrey, to which people used to come from
far away. Today, there are many good alternatives, but a mood of nostalgia and the
charm of Jaffa still linger at Andrey.

# 39__Green Ramat Aviv

*When the prime minister still lived modestly*

Green Ramat Aviv, as the area is known, has remained a modest area to this day. It was the first part of the northernmost city district, built in the 1950s. The houses that line ChaimLevanon Street, Brodetzki Street and Reading Street are still almost entirely single-storey and two-storey buildings. The green spaces that surround each house are linked by small paths. The district was planned in this way to enable residents to reach public buildings such as the local schools without crossing the road. It is worth taking a detour to explore these paths.

Most of the houses have never been properly renovated. This process has started only in recent years, and residents are able to apply for small extensions to their homes. There remains enough space between them in the green areas that point away from the road like fingers.

At the end of Reading Street the city authorities have laid out a small garden, Golda Garden, in honour of the former prime minister Golda Meir – the 'grey-bunned grandmother of the Jewish people'. She lived close by in a small road that runs parallel, Baron Hirsch Street, in one of its typical houses: single-storey, plain, modest. In view of the scandals of recent years relating to the enormous sums of money that today's politicians squander, it is hard to believe that a prime minister once resided here. A small wooden hut can still be seen on the site. There was once a security guard who sat here to keep an eye on things around Golda Meir. The outsized antenna on the roof is a further sign that someone who had to hold important discussions once lived here. Golda Meir moved into the house in 1959, when she already held the post of foreign minister. After the sudden death of Levi Eshkol in March 1969, she was chosen as his successor and served as prime minister of Israel for five years. In December 1978 Golda Meir died of cancer.

**Address** haBaron Hirsch Street 8, Tel Aviv – Ramat Aviv | **Getting there** Bus 6, 24, 25 or 45 to Reading / Brodetzky, or in the other direction to Reading / Asher Barash | **Tip** Hurshat Reading, a small wooded area on Reading Street, the site of the Alliance School, is a wonderful green refuge where the trees provide pleasant shade in summer. A large playground for all age groups with fitness equipment and an area for dogs are on the site.

# 40__Habash
*Ethiopian food in south Tel Aviv*

It is a little bit like entering a different country when you pass through the door of the Habash restaurant and are greeted by unfamiliar smells. Modelled on a hut in an Ethiopian village and decorated in matching style, Habash serves authentic Ethiopian meals that are also kosher.

The immigration of Ethiopian Jews, the Beta Israel, mainly took place in two dramatic operations in 1984 and 1991, when tens of thousands of them were brought to Israel in an airlift. Integrating them into Israeli society was a great challenge for the country. How far this was done successfully is a matter for discussion. Discrimination of dark-skinned Jews is certainly a common occurrence. For this reason, the intention at Habash is to bring Ethiopian immigrants and long-standing Israelis into closer contact by means of the Ethiopian culinary culture.

The main component of Ethiopian cuisine is the injera, a spongy, sour-dough flatbread, which at Habash is made from specially imported teff flour, i.e. flour made from a species of lovegrass native to Ethiopia. The injera serves as both plate and cutlery. The food is taken from a large dish and placed directly on the injera, then eaten using small pieces broken off from the bread. The large dish remains in the middle of the table, and everyone eats from it. Another aspect of the tradition is that guests present morsels of food to each other. The various items on the menu, called wot, are either based on pulses, especially lentils and chickpeas, or on meat, primarily chicken and lamb. When you come to this restaurant for the first time, the best option is to order one of the two mixed dishes. The drinks are either Ethiopian beer or tej, a kind of mead that is made in-house. And also, of course, Ethiopian coffee, buna, which is roasted on site at Habash, and of which you should traditionally drink at least three cups.

Address haNegev Street 8, Tel Aviv – Neve Sha'anan, +972 (3) 5164264 | Getting
there Bus 1, 5, 40, 42 or 89 to Chevrat haChashmal/Derech Begin | Hours Sun–Thu
10am–10pm, Fri 10am–start of Shabbat, Sat end of Shabbat–11pm | Tip One street
to the south is the site of the old central bus station, for a long time "the lowest point in
Tel Aviv", according to a well-known song. The city government has now laid out a
playground here, but needles and condoms in the shrubs show that the old days have
not yet passed. If you want to look around, it is better to do so by daylight.

# 41__haBima Square

*Walk in the sunken garden*

Following a thorough renovation, the square in front of Israel's national theatre, haBima, has become a real embellishment to the city that is used intensively by the people of Tel Aviv. The haBima building was constructed between 1935 and 1945. In those days, its neighbour was still the municipal garden department, along with a field that was used for education in agriculture. The concert hall of the Israeli Philharmonic Orchestra and the Helena Rubinstein Pavilion for contemporary art were only added later, making the site, which occupies slightly elevated ground, into an arts centre. Most of the extensive square was used for a long time as a car park, however, which did nothing to enhance its atmosphere, to put it mildly.

This has changed. Comprehensive restoration work has been carried out, giving a new façade to haBima and adding an underground car park. The square, now free from cars, was handed over to the artist Dani Karavan for a new design. As at his Kikar levana (see ch. 55), Karavan here used various elements from the history of the site and created art that you can walk through, in which a leading role is given to nature: water, trees, lawns, stones and sand shape this urban masterpiece. Gan Yaacov, the park with its mature trees in the north-west corner of the square, was also restored.

Through this work, haBima Square increasingly became a place where people meet. In the afternoon parents of children flock to the square and enjoy the open space in the middle of the city. Their offspring can play on the paths and in the sand pits in Karavan's sunken garden. The square has begun to rival Rabin Square in recent years, and is also a space used for demonstrations and assemblies. During the social protests of summer 2011, when Rothschild Boulevard became a village of tents, the centre of the protest movement was here.

הבימה
התיאטרון הלאומי

Address Kikar haBima, Tel Aviv – Old North | Getting there Bus 5 to haBima / Tarsat, bus 39 or 63 to haBima / Sderot Ben Zion | Tip The terraced houses on Huberman Street on the eastern part of the site, built in the 1950s by Dov Carmi, used to be called 'chocolate houses', as some of them belonged to the owners of Elite, the company that made the famous 'cow chocolate' in Ramat Gan after 1934.

# 42__Halper Bookshop

*Second-hand heaven on Allenby Street*

You can find lots of cheap things in Allenby Street. Cheap clothes, cheap pubs, cheap striptease joints. The street lost its good reputation a long time ago, even though several cultural institutions such as the Mughrabi cinema once stood there. Today, Allenby Street is dirty and noisy, and full of dime stores. It is also an El Dorado for bookworms. Along the two kilometres from Rothschild Boulevard to the sea, about a dozen second-hand bookshops are scattered. Some of them are specialised, for example in Russian or Spanish literature, while others have a motley mix of stock among which it is often possible to discover a true gem.

Halper Bookstore is an especially good example. About two-thirds of the 50,000 volumes in the store are in English, but there are also French, Spanish and German books. The range of literature in other languages is much smaller than in English, but it is nevertheless a high-class selection: popular romantic fiction by Rosamunde Pilcher stands next to philosophical works by Walter Benjamin in perfect harmony.

Halper occupies the rear part of the building. Only a small glass case shows the way to the backyard. On the other hand, the shop, which is bursting at the seams, has been able to spread out in the yard, where more shelves and newspaper stands have been placed.

Yosef Halper, who immigrated from New Jersey in the 1980s and opened the shop in 1991, knows every single one of his books and is pleased to help. The four rooms are crammed from floor to ceiling, and customers have to pick their way through the maze. They can find every genre here, from novels, children's books and comics to travel guides and magazines. Halper also stocks an excellent array of non-fiction books covering almost every academic discipline. His customers include residents of Tel Aviv and tourists, academics and students, collectors and bargain hunters.

Address Allenby Street 87, Tel Aviv – City Centre | **Getting there** Bus 4, 17, 19, 31 or 72 to Allenby/Montefiori or Allenby/Maze | **Hours** Sun–Thu 9am–7.30pm, Fri 9am–4pm | **Tip** Next door is a synagogue founded in 1926. It belongs to the Moshav Skenim old people's home, but is no longer in use. The entrance is adorned with beautiful small ceramic plaques that you can examine more closely from the steps.

# 43__haMedina Square

*Where you can hang out next to luxury shops*

How about a smartphone cover for €5,000? If you think you really must have this, there will be no problem getting one in Tel Aviv – on haMedina Square, the city's address for luxury shopping.

Shoes, watches, kitchen equipment and of course clothes are on sale here, both from the big international labels such as Boss, Ralph Lauren and Gucci and from high-class local boutiques. To match this, among the parked cars that crowd the square the proportion of expensive marques, Mercedes, Audi and sometimes a Porsche, is much higher than in the rest of the city. The shops, interspersed with cafés, banks and a considerable number of hairdressers, line the road that surrounds the square. The street is named after the Hebrew date of the foundation of Israel, and this corresponds to the name of the square itself: State Square. In the past, it was used on official occasions for holding military parades. As late as 1970 there was a big display of tanks here on Independence Day.

None of this is in the air today. The square is, on the contrary, sleepy and quiet, because to leave the outer circle of luxury stores and reach the inner part of the great roundabout is to enter a completely different world. Local residents use the large area of grass, which is always dried-out in summer, as a place to have a picnic, do yoga and exercise their dogs. But the square is by no means full of people.

Most of the time this is a spot where you can enjoy solitude and the open space, but it is doubtful how long this will continue, as the city government is planning to build the next big eyesore here. At one particular time of year it is better to avoid the square: when hundreds of local children celebrate Lag baOmer here. At this festival in May, camp fires are lit that, in a country like Israel with few trees, are mainly made from old building materials – and therefore smell unpleasant.

Address Kikar haMedina, Hei be-Iyar Street, Tel Aviv – New North | Getting there
Bus 7, 14 or 22 to Kikar haMedina / Lipsky | Tip At the corner of Weizmann Street
and Beeri Street, some 300 metres south of haMedina Square, a statue of Eli Ilan and
name plaques in two languages honour the 11 Israeli athletes who were taken hostage
by Palestinian terrorists and killed during the Munich Olympics in 1972.

# 44 The Hassan Bek Mosque

*The historic border between Tel Aviv and Jaffa*

The mosque on haYarkon Street, not far from the dolphinarium, looks a little bit lost. Surrounded by hotels to the south and the large Carmelite car park, the Hassan Bek Mosque seems to have been removed from its proper context. And this is indeed the case, as it is one of only two historic buildings in the Manshiye district that were not demolished. The mosque bears the name of the Ottoman governor of Jaffa who ordered its construction from white limestone between 1914 and 1916. In those days, the mosque lay far from the Muslims of Jaffa, and Manshiye was still sparsely populated. By building it, the governor wanted to set a southern boundary to the Jewish settlement and demonstrate Ottoman sovereignty on the ground. The mosque, which thus lies on the historic border between Tel Aviv and Jaffa, has indeed been a place at which the Jewish-Arab conflict in the city has come to a head again and again. In the War of Independence, for example, Arabs used the minaret as a position for firing weapons, and Jews attacked the mosque several times, once in the aftermath of the attack at the dolphinarium (see ch. 29).

As Manshiye grew, its place of worship became the religious centre of this mainly Muslim quarter. After the War of Independence, it was abandoned, however. The colourful windows, doors and mosaic tiles were stolen and the building fell into decay. In the late 1970s it was announced that the mosque had been bought by a Jewish investor who wanted to turn it into a shopping centre. A storm of protest, not only on the part of the Arab inhabitants of the city, put a stop to this plan, and in the end the mosque was handed over to the Muslim community of Jaffa. In the 1980s the minaret collapsed and was rebuilt, gaining considerably in height in the process. Today, despite its location off the beaten track, it is in daily use as a place of prayer.

**Address** haKovshim 82, Tel Aviv – Neve Tzedek | **Getting there** All bus routes to Carmelite, including no. 17, 31, 63 or 66 | **Tip** The course of the historic border between Tel Aviv and Jaffa was approximately the line of unassuming Daniel Street to the north. In times of crisis and during the War of Independence, this border was guarded by soldiers.

# 45__The Herzl Graffiti

*A beard and a message on Rabin Square*

Fruit orchards once occupied this site. Later there was a swimming pool with the municipal zoo next to it. Rectangular Rabin Square in the city centre was not laid out in its present form until the mid-1960s, when the city administration offices were built at its northern end. Since then the Square of the Kings of Israel, as it was originally called, has been the backdrop for the country's biggest mass gatherings. In April 1977, tens of thousands celebrated the first-ever Israeli victory in the European basketball championships following the triumph of Maccabi Tel Aviv. In 1982, 400,000 people demonstrated here for the end of the war in Lebanon following the massacres of Sabra and Shatilla. On 4 November, 1995 Yitzhak Rabin was murdered here after a peace rally. The square was then renamed in his honour.

'If you will it, it is no dream', said Theodor Herzl, the founder of political Zionism, his utopian vision of a Jewish state in Palestine. Whether he would be impressed by developments in Tel Aviv, which, by the way, was named 'The Old New Land' according to the translation of his novel, is a different question. Herzl wanted the Jewish people to have normality, and he could surely never have imagined the divisions in society that were tragically revealed by the murder of Yitzhak Rabin.

After summer 2007, Herzl graffiti appeared in Tel Aviv. They draw the observer's attention to missed opportunities by changing the text: 'Lo rozim, lo zarich …' – 'If you don't want to, you don't have to …', as the letters beneath Herzl's portrait proclaim. Most of these graffiti have now been painted over, but here, of all places, on Rabin Square, they are still present. You can find them on lamp posts in the east and west corners of the square, showing Herzl as an admonishing icon of everyday life, reminding us that everything depends on ourselves.

**Address** Kikar Rabin, Tel Aviv – Old North; the lamp posts are at the corner of Frishman / Malkei Israel and Frishman / Ibn Gvirol | **Getting there** Bus 18, 25, 149 or 174 to Kikar Rabin / Malkei Israel | **Tip** A great place to sit and eat the irresistible Linzer cake from the brasserie in Ibn Gvirol is the eco-pool at the south-west corner of the square.

# 46 Hill Square

*A historic hill in the Old North*

If you cross Ibn Gvirol Street on Milano Square heading west, in Horkanos Street you have to climb a short but obvious slope. The surrounding buildings mean that you only perceive the topographical situation to a limited extent, and what was once a conspicuous hill is no longer very noticeable here. Today you see a modest garden that has a tiny playground and, on its northern side, a small waterfall. The garden is densely planted. To explore this spot, which is hemmed in by parked cars, you have to walk around the square, as its noteworthy feature is in the middle, and is approached from the south.

Terrace-like stone steps lead you through the vegetation and up to a marble commemorative column. It preserves the memory of the British army officer after whom the square was named, Major General John Hill, who crossed the river Yarkon at this place in the night of 20 to 21 December, 1917 with his brigade and attacked enemy positions in a decisive battle. The capture of this hill, which was strategically important because it commanded a view of the surrounding country, and other positions on the further bank of the river – the British forces crossed the river in three places that night – paved the way for their victory over the army of the Ottoman Empire. In World War I, Hill was part of the Egyptian Expeditionary Force, which was formed in March 1916 to lead British forces in Egypt.

The district around the square was not built up until the 1940s. Today, it is one of the favoured residential areas in what is known as the Old North of Tel Aviv. In the 1970s the square was remodelled and planted with vegetation. In this process, burial caves and remains of Jewish settlements dating from the fourth millennium BCE were discovered. One of these caves, closed off by metal bars, is clearly visible, though it is often 'adorned' by litter.

**Address** Kikar Hill, between Horkanos and Shimon haTarsi Street, Tel Aviv – Old North | **Getting there** Bus 5 or 11 to Sderot Nordau/Yehoshua Bin Nun, then a few minutes' walk north through Yehoshua Bin Nun; bus 25 or 189 to Kikar Milano, then along Horkanos Street | **Tip** Five minutes' walk west you reach busy Yermiyahu Street with its small boutiques and cafés. Hummus Ashkara at 45 Yermiyahu Street is definitely the best hummus restaurant in the north of the city, and therefore well frequented.

# 47 Hotel Palatin

*Luxury accommodation for the Yishuv*

It was the first hotel in Tel Aviv – not a small guesthouse but a large, proper, high-class hotel. The first luxurious place to stay the night. It did not, however, stand where the giant hotels are today, lined up along the beach, but close to Rothschild Boulevard, at the crossroads of Ahad haAm and Nachlat Binyamin Street.

The need for a large hotel in the new city was already obvious in the 1920s. Dr Meir Masia decided to build one on his land and commissioned Alexander Baerwald, an architect from Berlin who had already designed several important buildings in Palestine, first and foremost the technical university in Haifa. Baerwald's aim was to evolve a particular style to suit the country, and combined a modern German kind of architecture with oriental characteristics. He did this at the Hotel Palatin, as the new accommodation was to be called. The name proclaimed what was intended: Palatin means palace. According to the rules, nothing higher than three storeys was to be constructed in Tel Aviv, but an exception was made for the Hotel Palatin, which thus became the tallest building by a long way. The grand opening took place on 31 August, 1926. The hotel had 60 rooms for guests, all modern with hot and cold water in the guest rooms, a roof garden and a ballroom. The waiters wore tailcoats and gloves to serve customers – it was an island of European style in the Middle East.

After the owner's death, the hotel continued to operate for a few years, but was then converted to an office building, a hotel and a club for soldiers, and later back to an office complex again. In 1993, it was given a thorough refurbishment, gaining an extra storey and a dome, as well as being painted in a strange colour that does it no favours. Today it stands at the crossroads, an oddly unfitting giant, but it is still possible to appreciate something of its former magnificence and grace.

Address Ahad haAm Street 28, Tel Aviv – City Centre | Getting there Bus 4, 16, 17, 25 or 31 to Allenby/Beit haKnesset haGadol | Tip A block further up at no. 110 Allenby Street, is the Great Synagogue, built in the same year and also the recipient of an unappealing façade following renovation. Baerwald proposed three different designs for the synagogue, all ultimately rejected. After a lot of toing and froing, he is said to have kept his vow never again to set foot inside this synagogue.

# 48 Hummus Abu Hassan

*Hummus or massabcha, that is the question*

Whether it is an Israeli or Arab dish is a matter for debate. And so is the question of whether hummus tastes better in Galilee or in Abu Gosh. But in Jaffa the status of Abu Hassan is in no doubt. In a small side street near the harbour, the best hummus, ful and massabcha are sold every day from eight o'clock in the morning until the pots are empty. The legendary founder of the business, Ali Karavan, who died in 2007, started out selling hummus from a hand cart in the Ayami quarter. Then he opened a small snack bar, and in the early 1970s he moved to Dolfin Street, which is still the location today. For 40 years and more Ali Karavan made the hummus himself, getting up at five o'clock every morning to cook the chickpeas. After refusing for years to open more branches, in the end he finally agreed. Today this hummus empire is run by Ali Karavan's sons. However, they have abandoned the experiment of opening a branch in Sarona (see ch. 83).

If you want to enjoy the authentic hummus experience, you have to pay a visit to the branch in Dolfin Street. You come here to eat – and only to eat. There is no time here for a social occasion. Even as you are being shown to one of the small tables, which you share with other guests, you place your order. By the time you have sat down, a plate has been placed in front of you, and as soon as you have eaten up, you vacate the seat for the next diners, who are already waiting. The queue goes all down the street, especially on Fridays.

The hummus here is wonderfully creamy. It is served with tahina and, if desired, ful, i.e. fava beans or broad beans. The truly divine dish, however, is the massabcha. In contrast to the recipe for hummus, for massabcha the chickpeas are boiled even softer but not pureed, instead being mixed with tahina and spices, then served warm. If you can't get enough of this, take a portion home with you.

**Address** haDolfin Street 1, Tel Aviv – Jaffa / Ajami | **Getting there** Bus 10 to Yefet / Louis Pasteur, bus 37 to Yehuda Margoza / Yefet | **Hours** Daily 8am – 2pm or 3pm (until nothing is left) | **Tip** If you would like to have more time, go to the branch at no. 14 Shivtei Israel Street. There are more tables here, as well as a more extensive menu including meat dishes and falafel.

# 49 __Hurshat Etzion

*A kibbutz on the southern edge of the city*

In the far south of the city, close to the border with Bat Jam, there is a small green area with a grove of trees ('hurshat' in Hebrew) between streets that are named after the philosophers Plato, Aristotle and Socrates. This place has an eventful history, with a story that begins far from Tel Aviv. In 1927, a group of orthodox Jews settled to the south of Jerusalem and established an agricultural community there. Only two years later it was destroyed by Arab neighbours. It was refounded in the early 1930s under the name Kfar Etzion, but had to be abandoned once again during the Arab unrest of the years 1936 to 1939. In the 1940s, finally, four religious kibbutzim – including Kfar Etzion – were founded, and were together known as Gush Etzion.

The United Nations partition plan designated the area as part of a future Arab state. Following repeated armed conflict between Jews and Arabs, in January 1948 all women and children were evacuated from Kfar Etzion. On 13 May serious fighting took place, the so-called Kfar Etzion Massacre, in which some 130 Jews were killed. After the foundation of the state of Israel, their widows and orphans settled in Jaffa in the Jabalia quarter, where they continued the life of the kibbutz, taking their meals and bringing up their children communally. The kibbutz was not dissolved until the 1950s. All that remains of it today is a small grove of trees, a little green island in the middle of a run-down residential area. The patch of green was once the courtyard of the kibbutz, and thus the place where most of its communal life happened. Some of the buildings, for example the former synagogue, which was both a religious and a cultural centre for the kibbutz, are still standing. A few years ago, the city authorities placed a memorial plaque at the entrance to the grove, telling the story of the kibbutz.

חורשת עציון
"החצר הגדולה"

"החצר הגדולה" הייתה מרכז חייהם של עשרות ילדים,
שפונו עם אימותיהם מכפר עציון במלחמת העצמאות -
תש"ח (1948). גוש עציון נפל בקרב, רוב הילדים התייתמו
מאבותיהם, אמותיהם התאלמנו. הם שוכנו בבתים העוטרים
את "החצר". בשנות ה-50 של המאה ה-20 ניטעה החורשה.
ברבות השנים השתקמו תושבי החצר, עקרו מכאן ובנו
חיים חדשים.

במלחמת ששת הימים, תשכ"ז (1967), נגאל גוש עציון.
בני כפר עציון זכו לשוב ולחדש בו את ביתם.
כאן טופחה מורשת גוש עציון וניטע גן החלום - "ושבו בנים
לגבולם".

ואתה, ההלך, מוזמן להעפיל להו ולחזות בהתגשמותו.

## THE COURTYARD

This courtyard served the widows and young orphans
of kibbutz Kfar Etzion who came to live in neighboring
homes after the fall of the Etzion Bloc on Nay 14 1948

---

**Address** Entrance opposite Aristo Street 8, Tel Aviv – Jaffa / Givat haAliya | **Getting there**
Bus 10, 37 or 41 to Yefet / Yotvat | **Tip** The nearby beach in Givat Aliya, as Jabalia is called
in Hebrew, is a good alternative to the overcrowded beaches of Tel Aviv. Here you can still
find the original coastal flora, as well as crabs and other animals of the shoreline.

# 50_Independence Hall
*'Like all other nations ...'*

This image is engraved on the collective memory of Israelis: David Ben Gurion, standing at a long table between his ministers, proclaiming the foundation of the state of Israel on 14 May, 1948. 'This right is the natural right of the Jewish people to be masters of their own fate, like all other nations, in their own sovereign State', he read from the Declaration of Independence. The city museum, once the home of Tel Aviv's first mayor, Meir Dizengoff, who is commemorated with a statue in the middle of the boulevard in front of the house, was sparingly decorated, the platform was furnished with one plain table, and the invited guests sat on simple wooden chairs. In the museum today you can gain an impression of the atmosphere of those days. The room is still preserved as it was then, and you can imagine the spirit of a new dawn that existed in May 1948.

For many years, the museum was in a sorry state. The colours on its information panels were faded, and the extremely conservative exhibition was unattractive. In 2009, it was finally decided to renew it and restore the House of Independence to its old splendour. The museum will then be housed over three floors. Much has to be done before it is finished, and at present only the room on the ground floor is open to visitors.

A new small feature can be seen above the passage through to the main room: during renovation, a ceramic plaque by the artist Chava Samuel was found. This simple plaque, decorated with a menora, naming the room as the place where the independence of Israel was proclaimed, was covered up by a wooden board for decades. Chava, the daughter of a rabbi from Essen in Germany whose real name was Eva Samuel, immigrated to Palestine in 1932. She was then already a trained ceramic artist. She worked in a studio in Rishon leZion and was among the founders of the ceramic art of Eretz Israel.

**Address** Sderot Rothschild 16, Tel Aviv – City Centre | **Getting there** Bus 3, 31 or 72 to Allenby / Sderot Rothschild, in the opposite direction to Allenby / Ahad haAm, bus 4, 16, 17, 25 or 31 to Allenby / Beit haKnesset haGadol | **Hours** Sun – Thu 9am – 5pm, Fri 9am – 2pm | **Tip** A little further on in the middle of the boulevard is a monument to the founders of the city, with the names of the 66 families who belonged to Ahuzat Bait. It stands on the site of the settler community's first well.

# 51__Independence Park

*Between the sea and the agave jungle*

Independence Park has had a lot of ups and downs in its history. The area, once the site of a Muslim cemetery, was marked as a park on the very first masterplan of the city. Then the army moved in, and the park was not inaugurated until 1952.

In its early years it was the city's largest park, laid out in the style of an English landscape garden with well-tended lawns and various sculptures – a real gem at first. In the early 1960s the remains of the Muslim cemetery were removed to make way for construction of the Hilton Hotel. Despite objections from the Arab population and from those who protested for aesthetic reasons, the hotel was built in the middle of the park. In allowing this the city authorities bowed to pressure from the government of Israel, which wanted to attract the international hotel chain to the country. Since then the park has been divided into two parts, which is not to its advantage. Over the years it fell into neglect, becoming dirty, overgrown and a rendezvous for cruising homosexuals.

Independence Park has played an important role in the homosexual culture of Israel, and has been commemorated in, for example, Yossi Avni's book *The Garden of Dead Trees*.

Following the restoration of the southern section of the park back in the 1990s, the northern part was given a comprehensive facelift in 2009. Now the park is once again an embellishment to the city, a place that can be explored by the whole family. From the limestone cliffs, which are up to 20 metres high, there is a wonderful view across the sea, stretching as far as Jaffa. The vegetation of the park is also well worth attention. It includes agave cactus, tamarisks, prosopis trees and many different kinds of fountaingrasses. Numerous statues, the mosaic fountain and a playground make Independence Park an inviting place to stroll and stop for a break.

Address haYarkon Street between Kikar Atarim and Sderot Nordau, Tel Aviv – New North | Getting there Bus 4, 9 or 13 to Ben Yehuda/Jabotinsky | Hours Accessible 24 hours | Tip At the corner of Jabotinsky/Ben Yehuda Street is a branch of Café Benedict that has been extremely popular in recent years, especially among night owls. Here you can breakfast round the clock, seven days a week, in the English, American, French or of course the Israeli style, sweet and hearty.

# 52 The Joseph Bau House
*A wide world behind a narrow door*

He was a painter, graphic artist, draughtsman, designer, writer, poet and pioneer of animated films in Israel: when Joseph Bau died in 2002 he left a huge legacy, the fruit of his highly creative life's work. His two daughters, Hadassa and Zlila, have made it into a small museum that is as colourful as Bau's own life was.

Joseph Bau was born in 1920 in Cracow. He survived the Shoah, not least due to his skills as a graphic artist, which the Nazis exploited. From the ghetto in Krakow he was deported to the labour camp at Plaszow, where he secretly married his beloved Rebecca; from there he was taken to the Gross Rosen concentration camp, and then, as one of those saved in 'Schindler's ark', to the labour camp in Brünnlitz. After the war he completed his studies at the Krakow School of Art. In 1950, partly because of the virulent anti-Semitism in Poland, he decided to emigrate to Israel with his family. For 40 years he worked in his studio in a small side street off Rothschild Boulevard. Here Hadassa and Zlila have preserved his working environment, his desk with its instruments for drawing and the projectors he used for his animated films. A true all-rounder, he simply made them himself. The walls of the small apartment are filled with Bau's drawings and pictures. The sisters are pleased to explain the background and how they came to be created. The special characteristic of Joseph Bau's work is the humour that is evident in it, even in drawings that were made in ghettos and concentration camps. There is also a lovely cycle about the Hebrew language, which Bau had to learn after emigrating. Although the museum is small, it is worth taking time for it, because leafing through all the catalogues and books will detain you just as long as listening to the entertaining stories that Bau's daughters tell about their fascinating father.

**Address** Berdyczewski Street 9, Tel Aviv – Old North, www.josephbau.co.il/house.html | **Getting there** Bus 5 to haBima/Sderot Rothschild, bus 39 or 63 to haBima/Sderot Ben Zion | **Hours** By arrangement, +972 (54) 4212730 (Hadassa) or +972 (54) 4301499 (Zlila), clilabau@gmail.com | **Tip** Around the corner at Rothschild Boulevard 140 is Tel Aviv's stylish variation on the pizza snack bar. The pizza at Tony Vespa, open daily from noon to 4am, is not the cheapest, but the thinnest, crispiest and perhaps the best in town, with typically Israeli toppings such as aubergine and artichokes.

# 53 Julie's Restaurant
*Tahrir Square is just behind the market*

'Make yourselves at home', says Julie warmly. And this is not difficult in her small restaurant, which is furnished like a living room with a white glass cabinet, pictures of family on the walls and all kinds of charming details. There are no more than 10 tables outside and inside, with pretty plastic tablecloths and a colourful mix of chairs. When her restaurant had to make way for new buildings after 12 years in Shabazi Street in Neve Tzedek, Julie Ozon moved to Malan Street in Kerem haTeimanim, the quarter around Carmel Market. Coming from the market, when you turn into Malan Street you first have to pick your way through the rubbish from the market stalls to reach the attractive lanes that are now coming to life in this district. In fact, this is a much better spot for Julie, in purely culinary terms, and her regular customers have remained loyal to her.

This is not surprising, because Julie knows what she is doing. She came to Israel with her family from Cairo in 1949, and now cooks authentic Egyptian meals, simple and extremely tasty. Every morning she decides what is on the day's menu, buys the ingredients in the market, and sets to work. Her guests can then come to eat between 11.30am and 4pm. Julie's daughter is often present too, and helps her mother. There is no menu. Instead of this, diners can simply come into the kitchen, see what is in the pots and pans, and then order the meal they would like. There are always different kinds of meatballs or fishballs, stuffed vegetables, vegetarian dishes and spicy dishes. If you like your food especially spicy, you can have an extra helping.

Julie sometimes chats with her guests, for example about developments in Egypt or other current affairs. She likes to talk, but she doesn't force herself on you. 'Julie's Tahrir Square' says a sign between the family photos. Who would have thought it was so close?

**Address** Malan Street 42, Tel Aviv – Kerem haTeimanim | **Getting there** Bus 4, 16, 22, 31 to Allenby/Bialik, then through the market or the little side streets | **Hours** Sun – Thu 11.30am – 4pm | **Tip** If you have a sweet tooth, go to the Halva Center at Carmel Market, haCarmel Street 5. They sell halva in excellent quality of all kinds, with nuts or – really delicious – with pistachios, chocolate or dried fruit.

# 54__Katzir Engravers

*How does the alef get on the keyboard?*

Everyone who buys a computer outside Israel and wants to type on it in Hebrew, is familiar with the problem: you have no great difficulty in switching the input language to Hebrew, but unfortunately operating the keyboard then becomes a guessing game. You can buy little stickers for a very reasonable price and laboriously stick them on the right keys. But when, eventually, the weather gets a bit warmer, the adhesive letters slip while you type or even attach themselves to your fingers. The solution to this problem is to be found in the south of Tel Aviv, in Chlenov Street.

Here, in an inconspicuous location between an electric goods store and an egg shop, is a tiny engraver's workshop. Two brothers, Moshe and Haim Katzir, have been in business here for 25 years. Their business is letters. They can engrave letters on computer keyboards in every language you can think of: in the Hebrew, the Russian and of course the Latin alphabet, as well as all the special characters in various languages, such as the accents, dots and lines on German, Scandinavian or French symbols. The brothers are the official letter engravers for several leading computer makers.

But even small customers can go to them with a laptop or a keyboard, which is then quickly taken out of your grasp. Before you can even protest, the keys have been removed. The letters are engraved on a machine one after another, then coloured. Finally, they are replaced on the keyboard. Moshe and Chaim tell a few funny stories while this happens, and obviously enjoy customers' praise for their precise work. In less than half an hour you can leave the shop again with your adapted keyboard, and no longer have any excuse for not writing in Hebrew. The brothers can also engrave any kind of sign, so you could, for example, get them to make a Hebrew name badge for you.

Address Chlenov Street 15, Tel Aviv – Neve Sha'anan | Getting there Bus 3, 19 or 25 to haAliya/Wolfson, then along Matalon Street to Chlenov | Hours Office hours Sun–Thu, +972 (3) 6870631 | Tip In Chlenov, formerly a worker's district that was built in the 1920s, a few interesting galleries have been founded in recent years: Chlenov 3 in a former picture-framing shop, the Binyamin artists' collective at no. 28 Chlenov Street, and above all the Hezi Cohen Gallery at Wolfson Street 54 are worth a visit.

# 55 Kikar Levana

*Landscape art with a stunning view*

At the end of La Guardia Street, between the busy feeder roads Derech haShalom and Derech haTayassim, there is a hidden oasis of peace with one of the city's most impressive works of art. It is not wholly visible from below, so you have to climb the hill in Edith Wolfson Park, which is the highest elevation in Tel Aviv, to reach the 'White Square'. This large-scale piece of landscape sculpture, designed by the internationally renowned artist Dani Karavan, has adorned the park since 1989 and is an invitation to visitors to walk around it.

As a reference to the White City, the work symbolises Tel Aviv and its foundation. It consists of a rectangular surface on which seven geometrical shapes in white concrete have been placed. A stepped square sunk into the ground corresponds to the surface area of a plot of land in Tel Aviv's first residential quarter, Ahuzat Bait. Next to it rises a pyramid, which is open on one side so that the sunlight reaches a marked line at midday. A domed building is split by an olive tree, which stands for the vegetation of this region, just as a channel of water divides a stepped building and the main flight of steps. A 20-metre-high tower, within which is an old alarm bell that could not be moved aside, provides a wonderful view of the city. If the door is locked, the park keeper at the entrance will be able to help. The installation is completed by a sundial set into the ground.

At weekends the park, with its wide expanses of grass, big playground and artificial lake, is inundated with visitors, who climb, slide, hop around, play hide-and-seek or do tricks on their skateboards. If you like some peace and quiet, it is better to come here on a weekday, but on the other hand it is wonderful to see how Karavan's sculpture becomes a huge area for play and how great art is an experience in the true sense of the word.

Address Between Derech haShalom and Derech haTayassim, Tel Aviv – Ramat haTayassim | **Getting there** Bus 23, 31, 34 or 39 to La Guardia/Derech haTayassim | **Tip** If you want refreshments, try Café Shaked at no. 40 Aluf David Street, which is part of Ramat Gan. Shaked serves simple but delicious and fresh meals, and is a well-known institution in the district.

# 56 Kiryat haMelacha

*Tel Aviv's mini Soho*

Artisans' workshops, department stores, cheap clothing shops, car-repair garages, bustling activity by day and dubious characters by night. This is the scene in what is currently Tel Aviv's artistic powerhouse. In recent years, many artists have moved into the Kiryat haMelacha 'artisan quarter', often sharing studios, attracted by the loft character of the premises and the low rents. Although the latter are now a thing of the past, the community of artists nevertheless continues to grow.

Kiryat haMelacha was constructed in the 1960s on the initiative of Mayor Mordechai Namir. It is not a pretty district. Its large, factory-like buildings, each of them entered from two sides, are ugly lumps of concrete. Four small parallel streets with inspiring names such as the Way of Power and Factory Way run through the area. It is all a little reminiscent of New York's Soho, although on a smaller scale, of course. Whatever you think of it, artists and gallery owners discovered the potential of the premises that can be rented in the Kiryat: high ceilings, naked brick walls, minimal furnishings, which is ideal for studios.

The long-established Rosenfeld Gallery, previously based on Dizengoff Street, was the first to take this bold step in 2009, when it moved to the Kiryat. Today, there are many galleries in the quarter, all of them specialised in contemporary art, including the Raw Art Gallery, Feinberg Projects and ZIZ. The Shpilman Institute of Photography is a venue for changing exhibitions, as well as regular discussions with artists and readings for specialist audiences. On certain occasions, for example the annual event called Houses from Within in May, the general public can visit artists in their studios. You can even admire art out on the street. In Kiryat haMelacha, leading Israeli street artists such as Klone and 0 Cent have left their traces.

Address Access via, e.g., Shvil haTnufa; the district is situated between Schocken, Kibbutz Galuyot and Sderot Har Zion, Tel Aviv – Herzl Hill (Givat Herzl) | Getting there Bus 3, 19 or 72 to Schocken / Derech Kibbutz Galuyot | Tip After so much modernity, something traditional is a welcome change, so eat at Shmulik Cohen, which has been serving good, down-to-earth Jewish food since 1936: gefilte fish, chopped liver, the inevitable chicken soup, tongue and much more, at no. 146 Herzl Street, a few minutes' walk north of Kiryat haMelacha.

# 57 _ Kiryat Meir

*A garden estate in the garden city*

When the first residents moved into Kiryat Meir in September 1936, they were founding the easternmost district of Tel Aviv. Surrounded by fields and plantations, the estate named after Mayor Meir Dizengoff, who died that very month, was a counterpart to Meonot Ovdim (see ch. 17) for the middle classes. The construction work was planned and carried out as a private initiative of the businessman Shalom Pechter. He bought the land that lay between the Arab village of Sumeil (see ch. 95) and the Templers of Sarona (see ch. 83), and published a building prospectus in early 1934 that included attractive loans. Some 700 people declared their interest within just a few days. A draw had to be held to decide who got the 170 apartments, almost all of them, that were then built.

The architect of this development in the International Modern style was Judith Stolzer Segal, who was born in Russia and grew up in Germany. She went to university in Danzig (now Gdansk), moved to Berlin in the late 1920s for her work and fled to Palestine in 1933. Her design, the winning entry in the competition that was held, included 12 buildings, of which 10 were completely identical, and stand in rows of two parallel to what is now Ibn Gvirol Street. The apartments inside them, too, all had the same plan, and were equipped with what were then state-of-the-art innovations such as a fitted kitchen with built-in cupboards.

At the two ends of the estate stand larger buildings. The long one with six entrances on Dubnov Street was constructed on stilts. Beneath it, steps lead to the garden, thus acting as a gateway to the estate. Today, you can still enter the garden by this route, as you can via the five parallel paths that cross the estate from Mane Street to Zeitlin Street. The garden is a wonderful urban oasis with a well-tended lawn, citrus and mulberry trees, and vegetable patches.

**Address** Between Ibn Gvirol, Zeitlin, Dubnov and Mane Street, Tel Aviv – New North | **Getting there** Bus 18 or 25 to Kikar Rabin/Malkei Israel, bus 89 to Kikar Rabin/Ibn Gvirol | **Tip** Dubnov Park opposite is one of the nicest in the inner city. It has a playground for various age groups and a large area of grass with trees to provide shade. The kiosk at the entrance is still run by the slightly eccentric son of the first owner, and has low prices.

# 58___ The Lighthouse
*The old look renewed*

There would seem to be nothing unusual about the fact that a lighthouse stands at the port of Tel Aviv. Nevertheless, it is often overlooked, possibly because of the huge size of its neighbour, the Reading power station. In fact, the lighthouse was built a few years before the harbour. The British erected it in 1934–35 at the mouth of the river Yarkon to warn passing ships away from the sandbanks. It is 17 metres high, and its light used to flash every 7 seconds.

During construction work on the lighthouse, the remains of the Tel Kudadi fortification dating from the 8th century BCE were discovered. It once served to guard the entrance to the river Yarkon. You cannot really see anything except for a small stony hill, and you have to use your imagination. At its centre a small column, like the one on Hill Square (see ch. 46), commemorates the crossing of the river here by British forces in the night of 20–21 December 1917 and their victory over the troops of the Ottoman Empire. The harbour was not built until 1936, when the general strike during the Arab revolt closed down the port of Jaffa. In 1937–38 the Reading power station was built. Next to it the lighthouse almost disappears, but it operated until the harbour was closed down in 1966.

Since then, the lighthouse has been left to decay, and its concrete is crumbling. It has served as a setting for several films, and has been immortalised in, above all, a key scene of the cult movie *Blues laChofesh haGadol* (*Late Summer Blues*).

In 2011, the tower was given a thorough restoration and repainted in its original chequerboard pattern, which brings out its features of the International Modern style very well. The viewing platform on the small extension building is unfortunately closed, and visitors are only admitted on certain occasions, for example the annual Houses from Within event.

Address Namal Tel Aviv, on the north bank of the Yarkon | **Getting there** Bus 4, 39 or 72 to Reading | Tip From the lighthouse there is a wonderful path for walking or riding a bike along the newly created Reading Park to the city's northernmost beaches, Tel Baruch and Hof haTzuk.

# 59   The Lobby of City Hall

*Tel Aviv at its most child-friendly*

When you think of Tel Aviv, what comes to mind is not necessarily a city made for children. The nightlife, sunbathing, high-tech industries – definitely not things for young kids. But in Tel Aviv, life is good for families, too. The city government makes efforts, and if more needs to be done, parents' groups and Facebook groups do intense lobbying. For some time now, Tel Aviv has been even more child-friendly: every Thursday between 4pm and 7pm, city hall opens its door for a relaxed afternoon of play. The entrance looks like a car park for baby carriages. And when you go up on the escalator, you can hardly believe your eyes: the counters are closed and roped off, and the whole lobby, the place where you otherwise stand in a queue to pay your property tax or a parking fine, is one big area for playing games.

The organisers have collected games from past times, games that many of today's iPad generation no longer know. However strongly the kids are addicted to their tablets, suddenly they have more fun here playing table football, skittles or an outsized version of Connect Four, piling up huge building blocks, and sitting on rocking horses. There are also balloons, a short theatre performance and make-up.

It is wonderful to see how the city government building, an ugly concrete monstrosity that was planned by a young architect, Menachem Cohen, in the mid-1950s in the style of the time, is taken over by the children. It would be difficult to imagine all this chaos in the offices of a European city. Of course, lots of things need to be improved, and of course there are some serious problems to be solved, as nursery groups with 35 children are much too large, and so are classes of 40 school pupils. Nevertheless, the city authorities are making an effort, and the Thursday afternoons are the best and also the noisiest demonstration of that.

Address Lobby of city hall, Ibn Gvirol Street 69, Tel Aviv – Old North | Getting there Bus 9, 25 or 189 to Iriat Tel Aviv/Ibn Gvirol | Hours Thu 4–7pm | Tip If you need some peace and quiet afterwards to let your hearing recover, go to the park behind the Gan-haIr shopping centre next to city hall. It is a reminder that there was once a zoo here, in the city centre.

# 60 The Lodzia Factory

*A heritage red-brick building*

At the intersection of Nachmani Street and Goldberg Street there stands a three-storey building of red brick, a style that is untypical in the White City. It looks more like an English factory. And indeed, the building known as the 'red house' was originally used for textile production. It was constructed in 1924 by Akiva Arie Weiss, one of the founding fathers of Tel Aviv, and designed by Josef Berlin, an architect from Russia. The building was named after Lodzia, one of the first manufacturers in the city, a company that made underwear. Its founders came from Lodz.

Each of the three storeys has a surface area of 370 square metres. The red-brick façade is punctuated by a large number of tall windows, and the roof is tiled. In the 1920s, this factory stood close to the Ottoman railway line between Jaffa and Jerusalem. However, in 1936 the company, now managed by Arie Shenker, moved to Holon. After that, the building was occupied by small workshops, then used as a warehouse. For decades it was then left empty, although the conservation office had listed it as a heritage building. Finally, in 2008 it became known that a businessman had bought it for 28 million shekels and planned to convert it into luxurious homes. Renovation work on this historic building has now begun.

This means that the fate of the factory building is the same as that of many others in the city that have been given the status of protected heritage. On the one hand, purchase by private owners for restoration is a great opportunity to save the buildings and renovate them. The disadvantage of this, on the other hand, is that the buildings are subsequently inaccessible to the public. The city authorities had required of the previous owners that one-third of the Lodzia Factory should remain publicly accessible, but this restriction on its use has now been abandoned.

**Address** Nachmani Street 43, Tel Aviv – City Centre | Getting there Bus 1, 40, 42 or 89 to Derech Begin / Nachmani | Tip Cicchetti at the corner of Goldberg and Yehuda haLevy Street is a kind of Italian tapas bar. The dishes are a mix of different items, all of them fresh and delicious. Then a Prosecco to wash it down.

# 61 Margoza

*The best bread in the city is in Jaffa*

Yes, the best pitta in Tel Aviv is from Abulafia. But if you want to buy some proper bread, you have to go a little further south to Yehuda Margoza Street. Here you will find a bakery and café with a family atmosphere called simply Margoza, after the street. Opened in 2009 by Michal, Zafrir and Shai, it sells baked goods in the French style. All three of them had their training and worked with the best pastry cooks and bakers in the city before they made their dream come true and set up their own bakery in Jaffa, in the immediate neighbourhood of the flea market.

In the last five years this district has undergone big changes. The whole street was renovated, and construction work continues. Many new shops have opened up as far as Yefet Street, most of them design and fashion boutiques but also more cafés. But don't allow yourself to be distracted by this, because Margoza is something extremely special.

The first reason for this is the quality of the products: sweet and savoury pastries, cakes, biscuits, confectionery, and especially bread. The genuine wholemeal and mixed-flour bread, but also the white bread, chala and rolls are all marvellous. The spelt bread is by far the best in town, heavy and full of goodness as only a proper wholemeal bread can be but at the same time light and airy, and easy to digest. The loaves can also be bought at other bakeries across the city – to find out where, it is best to ask at Margoza. Everything is baked here on the spot, with production going on all night, so a heavenly aroma pervades the alleys of the neighbourhood.

In the café you can also get sandwiches, salad and quiches, and if you want, you can also take everything home with you. If you do that, however, you will miss the cosy atmosphere of the café (not to mention the great coffee), which is small and intimate, attracting regular customers from far and wide.

חצי מלא
דגנים
לצא ושמרים
₪ 22

קמח מלא
100%
לצא ושמרים
₪ 19

קמח מלא
אגוז'ם
לצא ושמרים
₪ 22

70% שיפון
לצא ושמרים
₪ 19

70%
אגוז
₪ 19

עם
₪ 23

**Address** Yehuda Margoza Street 24, Tel Aviv – Jaffa Nord | Getting there Bus 10 to Yefet / Louis Pasteur, bus 37 to Yehuda Margoza / Yefet | Hours Sun – Thu 7am – 6pm, Fri 7am – 4pm | Tip It is always worth going to Shuk haPishpishim, a permanent flea market, where there is now a trendy mix of junk stores selling second-hand goods, old furniture and genuine antiques with new design shops.

# 62 — The Memorial

*For victims of air raids in World War II*

A year after the start of World War II, on the afternoon of 9 September, 1940, Italian warplanes bombarded Tel Aviv. Some 137 people were killed and more than 80 injured in the raid. The city and the Yishuv, the Jewish community in Palestine, were not prepared for this attack by an Axis power, which was primarily aimed at the British and their presence in the Middle East. The Italian air force had already made several attacks on Haifa, which had greater strategic importance due to its port. But nobody had expected a bombardment of Tel Aviv.

The worst damage was inflicted on Bograshov Street and Trumpeldor Street, where many tin huts and wooden huts stood at that time. They either burned down or were completely destroyed. The dead included Arabs, two adults and five children from Sumeil (see ch. 95), and an unknown Australian soldier. There was great outrage at the attack, as it deliberately targeted innocent civilians. A few days later the British Royal Air Force bombarded airbases on the Italian-occupied islands of Rhodes and Leros, from where the warplanes had taken off to attack Tel Aviv. In June 1941, the Italian air force carried out a second raid. This time 13 people died when Beit haInvalidim, a home for people with handicaps in Marmorek Street, was hit.

In 1995, the city government of Tel Aviv inaugurated a memorial stone for the victims of the Italian bombing raids. It bears the names of all those who died. Nevertheless, these events have largely been forgotten today, presumably because too much has happened since then in the state of Israel, which was founded shortly after these events, and memories of World War II have been buried beneath later happenings. The stone can be found on the eastern side of Mikhoels Square at the intersection of King George Street and Ben Zion Boulevard. It lies on a small area of grass with benches.

**Address** Mikhoels Square, Tel Aviv – Old North | **Getting there** Bus 18, 25, 61 or 72 to haMelech George / Beit Jabotinsky, bus 39 or 63 to Sderot Ben Zion / haMelech George | **Tip** Next to the memorial is Osen shlishit (Third Ear), Tel Aviv's best video store, which also sells DVDs and CDs. In the Osen Bar in the same building concerts are held every evening.

# 63__ The Montefiori Water Tower

*The district where the lemon trees flowered*

Almost a dozen water towers remain in Tel Aviv today. They are relics of the days when the wells could no longer supply enough water for a constantly growing city. The Montefiori district demonstrates beautifully that these towers were more than merely practical infrastructure for the water utility, but proud symbols of the renewal of Jewish life in Palestine.

The Montefiori district originated in an agricultural initiative. In 1853 Rabbi Yehuda haLevi Margoza established a plantation that was irrigated by a well, over which the water tower was later constructed. Two years later the British philanthropist Moses Montefiori took over the land. In the early 1920s a residential quarter was built here, forming an independent community until 1943. Since then it has increasingly become a business district. The water tower was constructed in 1935. It is 15 metres tall, has a capacity of 110 cubic metres and is supported by six concrete pillars that are connected in such a way that when viewed from below, a Star of David can be seen. It was planned by the engineer Yaakov Zwanger, who was the subject of tragic news headlines when his body was found in the sand dunes of Tel Nof in 1937. He had been murdered. The background to the crime was a scandal about land speculation that was the talk of the whole Yishuv at the time.

The water tower has recently been restored. A few steps lead up from Ben Shamai Street, past the tower and a synagogue with fine glass in its windows, to the broad street Derech Menachem Begin. The entire Montefiori district is undergoing transformation at present, the result of which is strange mixture of new residential structures and shabby-looking car repair garages.

**Address** Beit Shamai Street 9, Tel Aviv – Montefiori district | **Getting there** Bus 1, 40, 42, 51 or 63 to Gesher Kalka / Derech Begin, then the path to the water tower between Derech Menachem Begin 100 and 102 | **Tip** Yehudit Boulevard may not be as grand as its big brothers Rothschild, Chen or Ben Gurion, but therein lies its charm. Café Montefiori at no. 21 Sderot Yehudit stays open until 11pm and serves as a neighbourhood pub in the evenings.

# 64 The Mosaic Fountain

*The history of Tel Aviv in small coloured stones*

Nahum Gutman, born in Bessarabia in 1898, immigrated with his family to Palestine in 1905 and later became a pioneer of modern art in the country. He was trained at the Bezalel Art School and evolved his own Eretz Israeli style, which is evident in his landscapes and portraits, as well as in a number of mosaic works. One of his most impressive mosaics can be seen today at the end of Rothschild Boulevard. It originally stood in front of Beit haIr in Bialik Street, which used to be the city hall. The work, whose official name is *Little Tel Aviv*, was a commission awarded to Gutman by the city authorities in the form of a fountain. It consists of pieces of glass measuring one square centimetre each. They form three large panels of varying height at the centre, around which are arranged 15 smaller images in a circle.

The large panels represent the biblical story of Jonah and the whale, the first residential district in Tel Aviv, Ahuzat Bait and the cedars of Lebanon that King Solomon caused to be brought to Jaffa. The outer circle recounts various stages in the history of the city, showing Jaffa's Andromeda rock from Greek mythology, the conquests of Crusaders and Napoleon, visits by Montefiori and Herzl, immigrants going ashore in Jaffa, coffee houses in Tel Aviv and the reading of the declaration of independence.

The mosaic fountain was installed in 1976 and remained in front of the former city hall for more than 30 years. In the course of general renovation work it was removed in 2008, with the agreement of the Gutman family, and following a period of deliberations was finally given an attractive new home at no. 3 Rothschild Boulevard. Through the construction of a new high-rise complex, a small public space was created there with benches and loungers, making it an inviting place to linger. Refreshments are available from the street café kiosk on the corner.

**Address** Sderot Rothschild 3, Tel Aviv – City Centre | **Getting there** Bus 18, 22, 38, 61 or 82 to Migdal Shalom / Ahad haAm | **Tip** In Rokach Street in Neve Tzedek stands the Nahum Gutman Museum. In addition to works by Gutman it holds changing exhibitions of young Israeli artists. For children, there are frequent workshops and holiday courses.

# 65 Nachal Pardessim

*Along one of Tel Aviv's last plantations*

In the city's high-tech quarter, of all places, you can set out on a pleasant trip into natural surroundings. RAD, Comverse, Radwin and other tech companies have establishments in Ramat haHayal in the north-east of Tel Aviv. A business district has grown up, especially around Raoul Wallenberg Street, that takes its character from mirror-glass high-rise office blocks. When you drive along here it is difficult to imagine that you can look at the last plantations in the city only a few streets further on.

At the cul-de-sac end of Korazim Street you can begin a walk to what is called Nachal Pardessim, the 'plantation river'. This name is derived from the location. On the east bank of this little watercourse, which actually has no name, lie the last citrus-fruit plantations within the city boundaries. Oranges, grapefruit and pomelits, the Israeli cross between grapefruit and pomelo, grow here. The plantations are privately owned, so it is forbidden to pick anything, but it is always possible that a fruit will happen to fall from the tree. You walk through fine-grained sand here, as the riverbed is usually dry. In winter, if there is a lot of rainfall, the river appears as if from nowhere. One section about 200 metres long has been restored to its natural state in recent years. The banks have been planted with native species that bloom wonderfully, especially between the middle of February and mid-April. An initiative by some residents of the district was responsible for the transformation of the 'wadi of Neve Sharett', as the watercourse is called. It was only after their efforts that the city authorities decided on the project for re-wilding the river bank.

You can follow the riverbed south, along the big car park of Atidim, for almost a kilometre, but after two bends it is better to turn back, as otherwise you will reach a busy road, route no. 4.

**Address** At the dead end of Korazim Street, Tel Aviv – Ramat haHayal / Neve Sharett |
**Getting there** Bus 6, 7 or 42 to Beit El, then 15 minutes' walk north-east to Korazim
Street | **Tip** On the park opposite the office buildings at no. 30 Raoul Wallenberg
Street is a reflexology path: a short circuit over stones of varying shapes set into the
concrete. If you walk the path barefoot, it is supposed to stimulate different reflex
zones, thus providing relaxation for stressed-out high-tech employees and others.

# 66__ The Nalaga'at Centre
*Please touch*

It all began with a drama workshop for the deaf-blind, led by Adina Tal, a Swiss-born Israeli actress and theatre director. The result of this event was a unique link-up, which means that Jaffa is now the home of the only deaf-blind theatre ensemble in the world.

The theatre group has been taking the stage successfully since 2002 under Tal's direction and with the assistance of translators. *Light is Heard in Zig-Zag* is the title of a performance that gained an enthusiastic reception, not only in Israel, but also in Europe, the USA and Canada. In 2007, the ensemble acquired its own home: an old warehouse at the docks in Jaffa was converted into the Nalaga'at Centre. Here the theatre group performs three times a week.

But the Nalaga'at Centre does more than this. In Café Kapish visitors encounter deaf waiters, to whom they give their orders after a brief introduction to sign language. Here the roles are suddenly reversed, and the hearing visitors are the ones who need instruction and help. The same principle is employed in the centre's Blackout restaurant, where diners are guided by blind waiters to take their meals in the dark – an experience that stimulates all the senses. Finally, the Nalaga'at Centre also runs workshops for companies, schools and other groups that wish to work on their forms of communication – a field that is quite clearly the Nalaga'at Centre's area of expertise.

The deaf-blind actors achieve the incredible on stage. They act, make music and dance, and it is difficult to conceive the nature of this interaction in a world of silence and darkness. The waiters in the café and restaurant also teach visitors a sense of proportion. Everything at Nalaga'at is inspired by a light touch in dealing with handicaps. This uninhibited approach and humorous attitude are surely the main reasons for the success of this institution.

מרכז נא לגעת

**Address** Retsif haAliya haShniya Street, Tel Aviv – Jaffa port, www.nalagaat.org.il |
**Getting there** Bus 37 to Namal Jaffo / Yehuda haYamit, bus 10 to Yefet / Louis Pasteur,
then down to the harbour along Yehuda haMargoza Street | **Hours** Ticket and table
reservations online | **Tip** A few paces south of the Nalaga'at Centre, at the entrance
to the port, a blue marble circle has been set into the ground giving distances:
5 kilometres from Jaffa to Tel Aviv, 65 kilometres to Gaza, 88 kilometres to Haifa,
110 kilometres to Amman.

# 67 Nanuchka

*A place that buzzes even without lamb kebab*

Some years ago, Nana Shrier demonstrated that Georgian cuisine is hip. Now she has to show that Georgian and vegan are mutually compatible, as animal products were excluded from her restaurant Nanuchka in February 2014. Since its opening more than 10 years ago, Nanuchka has become much more than a well-attended place to dine and a popular bar. It is a genuine institution that lives from the style and ingenuity of the woman who founded it.

To begin with, the surroundings at Nanuchka represent these qualities. Once inside, you feel you have been transported far back to bygone days. The whole restaurant is cosy, but furnished stylishly and with great attention to detail. Some time ago Nanuchka was forced to move from a protected heritage building to a new one with a glass façade. But even in the modern location of the restaurant, the paintings on the walls, glass showcases with all kinds of knick-knacks, the tiled and mosaic floor, comfortable chairs and armchairs, and of course the plates with a flower pattern, make you forget where you are.

Nanuchka was famous for its uninhibited atmosphere, which often encouraged guests to dance on top of the bar. Juicy lamb kebabs were devoured, and alcohol flowed like water. And then came a great surprise: Nana announced that she was going to switch completely to vegan food. This made Nanuchka the first established institution to take such a step and showed how far the vegan lifestyle is progressing in Israel. The chinkali pasties filled with lamb were replaced with chinkali made from tofu, the chatshapuri – traditional Georgian bread from yeast dough with a filling of sour cream, eggs and cheese – is now based on soya, and the kebab is no longer lamb but artichoke. In the end, everyone is satisfied after these changes – and alcoholic drinks still flow like water, and the guests still dance on the bar top.

Address Lilienblum Street 30, Tel Aviv – City Centre, +972 (3) 5162254 | Getting there Bus 3, 31 or 72 to Allenby / Sderot Rothschild, bus 4 or 16 to Allenby / Lilienblum | Hours Daily noon – 5am; it is advisable to book a table | Tip Lilienblum Street is an entertainment district with all kinds of bars, one next to another, from stylish cocktail clubs to rustic pick-up joints.

# 68__Nechushtan

*On the trail of the mythical snake*

The Eretz Israel Museum in Ramat Aviv, founded in 1958, is one of the country's leading museums. Its holdings mainly consist of archaeological and ethnic or folklore collections, and thanks to its large outdoor area it is a suitable place to take children. One of its most interesting pavilions is called Nechushtan and is devoted to the history of mining and working with copper in ancient Israel.

The area that had the greatest deposits of copper ore in the region was in Timna, lying a little to the north of present-day Eilat and now a national park. However, the mines there were not the copper mines of King Solomon described in the Bible, as was believed for a long time. Following major archaeological digs beginning in the 1960s, it is now known that the people who established mines to extract copper ore here from the 14th century BCE onwards were Egyptians and Midianites. These mine workings were up to 30 metres deep, and have been recreated in the museum. One of the copper-smelting kilns on display was brought from the excavations in Timna, while the others are reconstructions. Information panels explain how the complex process of extracting and smelting copper was carried out over 3,000 years ago.

Before the Egyptians left Timna, they built a temple to the goddess Hathor, which the Midianites later converted to a site for their own religious cult. In addition to items for use such as tools, weapons and jewellery made from copper, the excavations also yielded vases, statues and many cult items, which can be seen in the exhibition. A number of these exhibits represent a copper snake. This mythical symbolic figure can be linked to the pole with a snake that the Bible attributes to Moses and that was later set up in the temple. Its name consists of the Hebrew words for snake (nachash) and copper (nechoshet), combined as Nechushtan.

Address Eretz Israel Museum, Chaim Levanon Street 2, Tel Aviv – Ramat Aviv | Getting there Bus 7, 13, 25, 45 or 127 to Planetarium / Chaim Levanon, Reading / Brodetzky in the opposite direction | Hours Sun – Wed 10am – 4pm, Thu 10am – 8pm, Fri & Sat 10am – 2pm | Tip Anina in the Museum, open daily from 9am until midnight, is the only café anywhere in this area, and with its mixture of delicious Israeli and Italian dishes it has something to suit everyone.

# 69 _The Negative Trees

*The Rabin Center from below*

On a hill in Ramat Aviv with a wonderful view of Yarkon Park and the north of the city stands the Yitzhak Rabin Center. This by no means modest building can be seen from far away. Opened 10 years after the murder of Yitzhak Rabin, it holds an archive, a library and a research centre. The museum was inaugurated later, and is officially called The Israeli Museum. In 10 stages it relates the history of the state of Israel and the personal biography of Rabin in parallel, with many photographs and a lot of film footage, presenting the themes in a self-critical way and in connection with the historic turning points in the development of the country. The museum features on programmes of visits for school children and soldiers.

The entrance can be reached from Chaim Levanon Street, but if you do not arrive by car, then you can enter on the south side coming through the park. A pedestrian bridge takes you across busy Rokach Street. The path leading to the museum is flanked by inconspicuous yet impressive landscape sculptures by one of the most important Israeli artists, who is also internationally renowned: the *Negative Trees* of Menashe Kadishman.

The painter and sculptor Kadishman, who was born in 1932 in Tel Aviv and died there in May 2015, was famous not only for his colourful sheep paintings but also for sculptures cut out of thin sheets of steel. An intense exploration of nature is at the heart of his work. The *Negative Trees*, silhouettes of broadleaf trees cut out of steel, can also be seen in the Philbrook Museum of Art in Tulsa, USA, and in the Sportpark in Duisburg, Germany. Here in Tel Aviv they stand between genuine palms and olive trees, as if in their natural environment. The negative space formed by the cut-out tree shapes opens up a view like a window. The eight works thus provide different perspectives on the museum behind them.

**Address** Chaim Levanon Street 8, +972 (3) 7453313, www.rabincenter.org.il | **Getting there** Bus 22, 89 to Merkas Rabin / Sderot Rokach | **Hours** Sun, Mon & Wed 9am – 3.30pm, Tue & Thu 9am – 5pm, Fri 9am – 12.30pm; visits by arrangement | **Tip** Right next to the Rabin Center on Chaim Levanon Street lies the Palmach Museum, where the exhibition on the elite fighting force before the foundation of the state of Israel is idiosyncratically conceived, but nevertheless worth a visit. Here too, visits are by arrangement only: www.palmach.org.il.

# 70__Neve Schechter

*From a historic café to an arts centre with a synagogue*

The vision and stubbornness of Rabbi Roberto Arbib were mainly responsible for the founding in 2012 of the Neve Schechter Legacy Heritage Center for Jewish Culture. Based in Neve Tzedek for more than 20 years, this institution had long had its eye on a historic building that stood empty for many decades. The house on the corner of Eilat Street and Shlush Street was built in 1886 by the German Templer Franz Lorenz, who lived in the American Colony (see ch. 4). Bar mitzvas, weddings and even screenings of silent movies were regularly held in Lorenz's house. In the 1930s, meetings of local German supporters of the Nazi party also took place there. A café and a pub were housed on the ground floor and in the garden. The location of the house between Jewish Neve Tzedek and Arab Jaffa, and also the fact that it was managed by German Templers, created a unique atmosphere that long-standing residents of Tel Aviv still recall with nostalgia. During World War II the house was used as a mess for British army officers and after 1948 served the same purpose for the Israeli armed forces.

The restoration of the building was a lengthy process, but the effort was well worth the effort. The house was superbly modernised but at the same time its wonderful original details were retained. The vaulted ceilings and mosaic tiles take visitors back to a bygone era. Here Rabbi Arbib turned into reality his vision of a lively arts centre that represents the Masorti movement in Judaism. It is a venue for weekly workshops, live performances, art exhibitions and events for children. Café Lorenz can be booked for weddings and bar mitzvas. The beautifully adorned synagogue in Neve Schechter is also run according to the customs of conservative Judaism. Men and women pray and sit together here, for example, a practice that is attractive to many Israelis who live a secular life.

**Address** Shlush Street 42, Tel Aviv – Neve Tzedek, office@neve.org.il, www.neve-schechter.org.il | **Getting there** Bus 40 or 41 to Eilat/Shlush | **Hours** Programme of events on the homepage under 'Exhibits' | **Tip** If you walk north along Shlush Street you soon reach a small bridge. The canal-like open space beneath it, now used as a car park, is the course of the historic railway line from Jaffa to Jerusalem.

# 71__Neve Sha'anan Street

*A pedestrian zone through a different Tel Aviv*

In the south of the city, around the central bus station (see ch. 5), lies one of the shabbiest districts of Tel Aviv. The people who live here are mainly migrant workers and African refugees, especially from Sudan and Eritrea. After dark, crime, drugs and prostitution are prevalent in the area. If you would like to get to know the darker side of Tel Aviv, in daylight hours you can do so without difficulties, however.

The district was founded as a consequence of the unrest in 1921, when Jewish residents, fearing further acts of violence with the character of a pogrom, left Jaffa. Four hundred people formed a community that they named Neve Sha'anan and acquired a large plantation to build a new residential quarter. The development plan envisaged streets and parks in the shape of a menora, the traditional Jewish candelabrum. In the end, this idea was not implemented in full, but a glance at the map of Tel Aviv clearly shows part of this menora. Among the streets that run in a parallel curve between Levinsky and Salomon Street is Neve Sha'anan Street, today a pedestrian zone.

You can still spot a few of the houses that were once typical of this quarter, including some tiny ones that originally consisted of just two rooms, for example at the corner of Rosh Pina Street, as well as some plain ones built in the International Modern style such as the Karmin House at number 23. What they all have in common is that they are in a state of terrible decay and accommodate shops and businesses that reflect all the diversity of the nations that come together here. The best time to experience the colourful bustle is on a Friday afternoon. When things get quiet in the rest of Tel Aviv, things are at their liveliest here. Goods are then offered for sale on carpets, as at an open market – everything from small electrical items and toys to spices and stolen bicycles.

**Address** Neve Sha'anan Street, Tel Aviv – Neve Sha'anan | **Getting there** All lines to the central bus station, e.g. 4, 5, 54 or 89 to Tachana Merkasit | **Tip** Levinsky Park is a rendezvous for African refugees, in some cases their home. Around the library in the park established by volunteers you can gain an impression of this situation.

# 72__The Noga Quarter
*Coffee roasting and young designers*

One of the districts that has changed most in recent years is the Noga quarter in the north of Jaffa. Spectacular renovation of old buildings and construction of new ones between Jerusalem Boulevard and the American Colony ushered in the gentrification of this area. There are still some run-down buildings and places, but the trend has become irresistible. Around modest Segula Square and in the side streets running off it there have appeared many design shops, making the Noga quarter an El Dorado for beautiful things.

Most of these stores sell clothing, jewellery and shoes, but furniture and other items for the home can also be found, alongside the little old workshops of tailors and upholsterers. This does not necessarily mean that two different worlds collide here, as many of these young Israeli designers also have their studios attached to the boutiques, which means that they are performing artisan work on site. Sometimes you can watch them at work.

The district takes its name from the Noga Hall on Jerusalem Boulevard, where there was once a cinema. It was opened in 1922, then bearing the name of its Arab owner, Nabil. After 1948 it became the Noga Cinema. Today, this is the home of the Gesher Theatre, which was established in 1991 by Russian immigrants. A wide repertoire is staged here, with performances in Hebrew, but with Russian and English subtitles.

The time to meet on Segula Square at the heart of Noga is Friday morning. It is a rendezvous not only for local residents, but also for visitors from across the whole city, as it is definitely hip to kick off the weekend here. The excellent coffee to match this trendy scene is available from Cafelix, a small, popular café run by a German and his Israeli wife, who roast and grind their own beans. While parents drink coffee, their children can slide and climb on a small playground.

Address Ruchama, Sgula, Tirtsa Street and the side streets, Tel Aviv – Jaffa Nord | Getting there Bus 11, 18 or 37 to Prof Kaufmann / Goldman | Tip The Avni Institute in Eilat Street is Tel Aviv's oldest school of art. Founded in 1936, it is one of the most renowned institutions in the country. Every year in July the work of the graduating classes in all disciplines is exhibited in the rooms at Eilat Street 23.

# 73__The Old Cemetery

*Tracking down the Jewish history of Jaffa*

It is worth visiting the old Jewish cemetery in Jaffa for the view alone. On sunny days, there is a wonderful play of colour between the pale gravestones, the clearly delineated blue horizon that is so characteristic of the Middle East and the even deeper azure of the sea below. But above all, the cemetery reveals a great deal about the Jewish settlement in Jaffa in the 19th century. An area on elevated ground in the Ayami district was acquired by the Jewish population of Jaffa in 1834. At that time, this community consisted of only about 150 Sephardic Jews. Until then they had taken their dead to Jerusalem for burial on the Mount of Olives, which was a laborious and expensive undertaking.

In the 1830s the community began to grow. It increased further thanks to the immigration of Ashkenazi Jews, and flourished under Rabbi Yehuda haLevi Margoza, who from 1840 onwards was the chief rabbi of Jaffa. When the cemetery came into use, a chevra kadisha, the funeral society that takes on the task of ritual burial in the Jewish faith, was established for Jaffa. With a short interruption during a cholera epidemic, this cemetery was used for burials until the 1920s. After this time, the new Trumpeldor Cemetery was used (see ch. 100).

There are about 2,000 graves at the site, which has the popular nickname 'Ayami cemetery'. Only 805 gravestones remain, however, and the other graves are either anonymous or empty. The Ottoman government ordered the cemetery to be cleared at the start of World War I, and numerous graves were relocated. In addition to Rabbi Yehuda haLevi Margoza, many of the founders of the Jewish community in Jaffa from the period of the first great wave of immigration are buried here. One of them is Dr. Shimon Frankel, who came from Silesia. In the 1840s he opened the first Jewish medical practice in the country.

Address Entrance near Sheikh Bassam Abu Zayd Square at the junction of Yehuda Margoza and Yehuda haYammit Street | Getting there Bus 10 to Yefet/Louis Pasteur, bus 37 to Yehuda Margoza/Yefet | Hours Mon & Thu 8am–noon | Tip Follow the road to the sea and then turn south to reach the extensive Midron Park, adjacent to the large, free car park at the harbour. It is a beautifully laid-out park with wide lawns and playground and fitness equipment.

# 74 The Old Wall

*Stone testimony to the Templers*

Olifant Street, not far from Rothschild Boulevard, is one of the greenest thoroughfares in the city. Even in summer the dense foliage of old trees casts pleasant shade and creates the impression when you turn the corner that you have entered another country. In fact, this street has a history going back beyond the foundation of Tel Aviv, and stone remains of this can be seen here. At various points an old wall is visible between the houses, for example at number 14, but also further up the street. It is an inconspicuous, plain wall, and extremely crumbly in places.

It once bounded a large agricultural estate that existed here in the second half of the 19th century, long before Tel Aviv was founded. In this period, a number of attempts were made by Christians to settle the land, for example in the American Colony (see ch. 4). One of them, Konrad Röhm, bought the area between present-day Lincoln Street, Derech Menachem Begin Street, Olifant Street and Wilson Street from Italian nuns in 1870, and cultivated fruit and vegetables there. On contemporary maps this spot is marked with the name 'Röhm Hof'. Only two years after the death of Röhm and his wife, the farm was purchased by Johann Georg Günther, one of the German 'Templers', who also ran a bakery there. The site continued to be a plantation until after World War II. Then it was incorporated within the city boundaries, and sold by the Templers piece by piece. But even as late as the 1950s, a small field used for agriculture remained here.

Today, the school of art and a synagogue occupy this site. At the end of the street lies a small park with a playground, a good place to sit for a while. In Mazeh Street, the road parallel to Olifant Street, you can also find some remains of the old wall, for example between number 61 and number 63, if you go looking in one of the courtyards.

Address From no. 14 go up Olifant Street on the right; Tel Aviv – City Centre | Getting there Bus 23 or 70 to Yehuda haLevy/Sheinkin, bus 70 or 142 to Sderot Rothschild/Balfour, then along Balfour Street and Yehuda haLevy Street | Tip Taizu at Derech Menachem Begin 23 is a concept restaurant with unusual styling and high-class food inspired by chef Yuval Ben Neriah's travels in South-East Asia and the street food that he found there. It's not very cheap, but really good (bookings: www.taizu.co.il).

# 75__Oranger Suspendu
*The levitating Jaffa orange tree*

In the maze of alleys that is Jaffa's old quarter, you can discover a lot of art. Galleries line up one next to the other, and if you find your way to the south-east end and walk along Mazal Arie Street, through the arch of a gate you will see a tree that hovers a metre or so above the ground.

*Oranger Suspendu* is a landscape sculpture by Ran Morin that was installed here in 1993. The tree grows out of a seed-like vessel that is attached by cables to the adjacent buildings. When you touch it, the tree swings hesitantly to and fro.

This work of art commemorates the Jaffa orange, properly known as the shamouti orange, which was cultivated in Palestine from the mid-19th century and quickly became a major export. It is often seen as an element connecting the Arab and Jewish inhabitants of Palestine, as both groups of the population lived from growing oranges. The plantations around Jaffa disappeared long ago, and the export business is now controlled by Israelis.

The hovering tree is a monument to the Jaffa orange, but at the same time Morin's work is also a symbol of modern life in which humans and nature are divided and nature is artificial. The orange tree is a metaphor for modern humans, who grow towards an uncertain future, both rooted and uprooted at one and the same time. It is not easy to look after the orange tree. It needs the right soil and has to be watered carefully for it to survive – a little bit like the situation in outer space, says Morin. Nevertheless, the artist, who has created other levitating trees, has made the *Oranger Suspendu* so that it hovers in the narrow alley in a completely natural way, as if it could not possibly be any different. A small blue bench invites passers-by to stop and linger a while. As you sit there, you have the tree all to yourself, unless one of the groups that often visit on guided tours comes by.

**Address** At the junction of Mazal Arie and haTsorfim Street, Tel Aviv – Jaffa Old Town | **Getting there** Bus 10 to Yefet/Louis Pasteur, then Louis Pasteur Street towards the harbour and right into the Old Town along Mazal Te'omim Street | **Tip** At the end of Mazal Dagim Street the Ilana Goor Museum exhibits sculpture, photographs and many other design works by Ilana Goor and other Israeli artists, some of them well known, in a historic building with a lot of atmosphere.

# 76__The Pasáž Bar

*Beer in the underworld*

The Pasáž Bar is not simply called after a passage, it really is located in one: an underground passage, by day an extremely dreary place although it was once lively. The building at number 94 Allenby Street is noticeable primarily for its wide flight of steps leading downwards. There used to be bookshops and stores selling household goods here. Today the signs in the windows advertise an exhibition of postage stamps, and there is no sign of the old bustling activity. A few wobbly tables have been placed by a small kiosk that serves coffee.

At night, however, a metamorphosis takes place. The subterranean passage then becomes one of the hippest places in town, the Pasáž Bar. The steps are usually closed off, and the entrance is at the back. Apart from alcohol, the kiosk sells Japanese street food at reasonable prices, the number of tables is greatly increased, and the black table-tennis table in the background gets used. There is no air conditioning, but a few ceiling fans and a lot of electronic music create a steamy atmosphere.

The Pasáž Bar was founded by a party group called Nylon and the team from Radio EPGB, another underground music bar in a street running off Rothschild Boulevard. It has evolved, and is mainly a venue for concerts in a wide variety of musical genres, art events and modern-dance shows. It long ago ceased to be a strange and exotic location, now attracting well-known artists who can perform in laid-back surroundings here. The crowd who sit and stand at the motley mix of tables and chairs, whose style could charitably be described as vintage, is not all that young any more. This makes the Pasáž Bar a perfect place to go out for over-30s who want a little bit of culture with their beer. By the way, the toilets at Pasáž have what it takes to get cult status – definitely worth a visit, even during the daytime.

Address Allenby Street 94, Tel Aviv – City Centre, www.facebook.com/PasazAllenby |
Getting there Night buses 416, 418 or 463 to Beit haKnesset haGadol/Allenby, in the
opposite direction Allenby/Maze | Hours Irregular, just drop by on the off-chance |
Tip If you prefer things to be high-class, go a few houses further to Tailor Made. This
stylish bar occupies an old factory and attaches importance to interior design. Tailor
Made serves excellent food and a selection of its own cocktail creations.

# 77 _ The Pink Triangle Monument

*For the homosexual victims of the Shoah*

In January 2014, a remarkable monument was unveiled in Gan Meir. It deserves attention not only because there are very few such monuments in the world – they exist in, for example, Berlin, Amsterdam, San Francisco and Sydney – but rather because this was the first in Israel to commemorate non-Jewish victims of the Shoah. Designed by Yael Moriah, a landscape architect and professor at the Technion in Haifa, the monument stands right next to the entrance to the gay and lesbian arts centre. It consists of three pink blocks of concrete that resemble a shattered triangle, a reference to the pink triangle that homosexual inmates of concentration camps were forced to wear.

In three languages, Hebrew, English and German, the following words can be read on each side: 'In memory of those persecuted by the Nazi regime for their sexual orientation and gender identity'. Next to it an inscription explains the persecution of homosexuals by the National Socialists. About 15,000 people were imprisoned in concentration camps because of their sexual orientation, and more than half of these were murdered. In particular, homosexual Jews such as the sex researcher Magnus Hirschfeld are commemorated here.

In Israel's prominent memorial environment, this monument is an important milestone that puts the spotlight on otherness. And that is a good thing. Tel Aviv is, indeed, one of the world's gay-friendliest cities, but even here 2 people were killed and a further 15 injured in 2009 when an attacker opened fire in Bar-Noar, the Tel Aviv branch of the Israeli LGBT association. In the Middle East, where homosexuals are still persecuted, arrested and even executed, Israel and Tel Aviv in particular are a kind of oasis. It is therefore an extremely fitting site for the Pink Triangle monument.

DEN OPFERN DES NATIONALSOZIALISMUS. DIE WEGEN IHRER SEXUELLEN ORIENTIERUNG UND GESCHLECHTLICHEN IDENTITÄT VERFOLGT WURDEN

**Address** Gan Meir, between King George and Chernichovsky Street, Tel Aviv – City Centre, in the south-west corner of the park | **Getting there** Bus 18, 25, 38, 61, 72 or 82 to Beit Jabotinsky / haMelech George | **Tip** The gay and lesbian community centre in Gan Meir is the best place to get to know the city's gay scene.

# 78__ The Pri-Or Photo House

*Charming nostalgia in black and white*

For 70 years, number 30 Allenby Street was the address of a 'zalmania', a photography shop where you could have your portrait taken. Its owner, Rudi Weissenstein, was one of Israel's best-known photographers. Born in Iglau in Moravia in 1910, he came to Palestine in 1936 and met Miriam Arnstein, who also came from Czechoslovakia. They got married and opened the Pri-Or Photo House in 1940. Miriam continued to run the business after Rudi's death, working there indefatigably every day until she died in summer 2011 at the age of 98. Her grandson, Ben Peter, has now taken over the shop.

Weissenstein's archive contains more than a million negatives of photos taken between the 1930s and the 1970s. His most famous shot shows the proclamation of the state of Israel, to which he was the only photographer to be invited. His photographs are mainly devoted to the social and cultural life of Tel Aviv, which no longer exists as it was in his day. It is a nostalgic experience to see the beach promenade in the days before it was lined by high-rise buildings, Dizengoff Square (see ch. 29) when it had not yet been spoiled by the bridge, and the first central bus station, much pleasanter than it is today, as well as scenes from the cultural life of the city and portraits of well-known personalities. In the shop you can leaf through postcards, prints and photographic books, chat with Ben Peter and admire part of the original archive. The National Library is now taking care of this and has started to digitalise the negatives.

The reason that the Photo House no longer stands in Allenby Street but in a side street is that Miriam Weissenstein fought in vain to prevent the demolition of the building, a campaign that is described in a superb documentary film entitled *Life in Stills*. However, the move has not done any harm to the special atmosphere at Pri-Or Photo House.

**Address** Chernichovsky Street 5, Tel Aviv – City Centre | **Getting there** Bus 3, 17, 19, 22 or 31 to Allenby/Yona haNavi, in the opposite direction to Allenby/Geula | **Hours** Sun–Thu 10am–6pm, Fri 10am–1pm | **Tip** Just round the corner at the junction of Allenby Street and Bialik Street is Café Bialik, a good place to eat and watch the comings and goings on Allenby Street. The café has a programme of live music every evening with established and new artists.

# 79 Rambam Square

*So what is eclectic style?*

The pedestrian zone in Nahalat Binyamin Street is known for its fabric shops and for the artists' market held here on Tuesdays and Fridays. To see its true attraction, however, you should raise your eyes a little. If you do this, you will notice the architectural gems that are assembled here. They are best explored from Rambam Square, the junction of Nahalat Binyamin Street and Rambam Street.

This neighbourhood was founded at the same time as Ahuzat Bait but did not merge with Tel Aviv until more than two years later. The buildings, mainly dating from the 1920s, were mostly constructed in the eclectic style, meaning they are a jumble of various influences. Among these, Art Nouveau has left easily recognisable traces, for example on the imposing Beit haAmudim at 12–16 Rambam Street. It takes its name from the columns that dominate its façade. When it was completed in 1927 it was one of the largest residential buildings in Tel Aviv. Today, it is home to one of the trendiest jazz clubs in the city, also known as Beit haAmudim, where live concerts are held daily.

Opposite it lies the haKadim House, also named after its façade, which is adorned by Greek-looking earthenware vases. Its architect, Seev Rechter, was later one of the leading exponents of the International Modern style in Israel. It is reported that he was not especially proud of the haKadim House, which he designed before undertaking his trips to Rome and Paris.

The building at number 18 Nahalat Binyamin Street to the south of the square has an interesting history, related to the evolution of the city. It was built in several stages after 1913. Originally it was a hotel, named Spektor after the man who owned it. After World War I, three artists opened a school of drawing there. One of them was Nahum Gutman (see ch. 64). Between 1921 and 1926 it was home to the Hadassah Hospital, the first hospital in Tel Aviv.

**Address** Junction of Nahalat Binyamin and Rambam Street, Tel Aviv – City Centre | **Getting there** Bus 17, 18, 23 or 25 to Allenby/Balfour, bus 61 to Allenby/Maze | **Tip** One of the nicest stands on the artists' market is that of the photographer Orit Bechar, who sells images of graffiti and street art from Tel Aviv printed on wood. These little ornaments are perfect souvenirs of Tel Aviv and its streets. The stand is a few paces south of Rambam Square at the corner of Mohiliver Street (www.orit-art.com).

# 80_ The Rokach House

*The heart of Neve Tzedek*

The first thing you notice are the sculptures of fat, naked women that stare at visitors from every corner of the building – in the courtyard, from the balustrade, in the garden. But the plump ladies only came here at a relatively late stage. The Rokach House itself, by contrast, was one of the first buildings in Neve Tzedek, dating from 1887. It takes its name from Shimon Rokach, who lived here with his wife Rachel and five children. At the same time, the house was a place of assembly for the neighbourhood. Today, it is a small museum that tells visitors about life in Neve Tzedek years before Tel Aviv was founded.

Shimon Rokach, born in Jerusalem, moved to Jaffa in 1884 at the age of 21 and soon founded the charity Ezrat Zion with his brother Elazar. One of its aims was to alleviate the shortage of housing in Jaffa. On land belonging to Aharon Shlush at the boundary to Jaffa, the society planned a Jewish residential quarter that was divided into 48 plots. The houses were built by a cooperative of Jewish families from Jaffa, and Rokach's was one of the first 10. Initially they were single-storey buildings, and more were added later. The Rokach House was even given a small copper dome.

Shimon Rokach, who also founded the first Jewish hospital in Jaffa and the first library (see ch. 11), died in 1922. His children donated the house to the community, but later it was left empty. In the early 1980s his granddaughter, the artist Lea Majaro-Mintz, took it over and restored it in the original style. Today, a small exhibition with historic furniture and utensils is devoted to life in the early 20th century. The whole house is also a gallery, not only for works by Lea Majaro-Mintz such as the fat ladies, but also for temporary exhibitions. Theatre performances about the history of Neve Tzedek and concerts also regularly take place.

Address Shimon Rokach Street 36, Tel Aviv – Neve Tzedek | Getting there Bus 40, 41 to Eilat/Shlush | Hours Sun–Thu 10am–4pm, Fri 10am–2pm | Tip At the other end of Rokach Street you will find the house of Aharon Shlush, built in 1907 and once one of Neve Tzedek's finest buildings (no. 32 Shlush Street). It did not stay in the family, and since 2014 has been undergoing renovation for private use.

# 81 Rosh Tzipor

*In the wild east of Yarkon Park*

If you have an above-average need for a natural environment, you only have to seek out the right corner of Yarkon Park. The less tidied-up part of the park, which gets along without mown lawns, is called Rosh Tzipor. Here the green areas are not looked after, but can grow as they please, interspersed with grasses and flowers. Picnic benches stand here and there like small islands. Barbecuing, prohibited in the rest of the park, is allowed here. Even though many people do not keep to the zones designated for the mass sport of grilling meat outdoors, here you can have a barbecue in style. There is a large and popular playground in the middle of Rosh Tzipor. Next to it is a little lookout hill from where you have a good view of the surroundings. In the morning and late afternoon, Rosh Tzipor is an El Dorado for cycling. The two-kilometre circuit is well used by mountain bikers and racing cyclists. Unfortunately, their behaviour is sometimes reminiscent of the way people drive on Israel's streets, so it is wise to take care. On the paths within the park, however, there plenty of places to walk undisturbed, even in the bike rush hour, and walkers can follow a short fitness trail. The small area of woods was planted in the 1950s and is now home to huge eucalyptus trees that rustle wonderfully in the wind. Next to it is haChava ('the farm'), where city dwellers can grow their own vegetables.

Rosh Tzipor means 'bird's head' after the shape that the rivers Ayalon and Yarkon have cut through the terrain – and this part of the park is an excellent place for bird-watchers. Various kinds of heron are always present, as well as many waterfowl and songbirds. In 2013 work started on construction of a bird-watching centre. While it remains unfinished, it is worth coming to the park at quieter times on weekdays just to enjoy being here and appreciate the natural surroundings.

**Address** Ganei Jehoshua/Yarkon Park, from the car park of haChava in Ramat Gan, Rokach Street, or via the pedestrian bridge in the park at the end of haRav Kosowski Street in Bavli, Tel Aviv – Yarkon Park | **Getting there** Bus 14 to haRav Kosowski/Steinmann, bus 42 or 67 to Derech Abba Hillel/Rokach (Ramat Gan) | **Hours** Accessible 24 hours | **Tip** On the other side of the Yarkon you can see the remains of Sheva tachanot ('seven mills'). Until the 1940s, a large grain mill operated here using water power from the river.

# 82 __ The Salonika Houses
## *The heart of the haTikva quarter*

The haTikva neighbourhood in the south-east of the city does not have a good reputation. It was always a poor residential area with many problems, and in recent years the conflicts connected with refugees from Africa have become extremely acute. Noisy protests, some of them physical, of the long-standing Jewish residents against the Africans, whom they accuse of theft, violence and sexual assaults, are directed against refugees from states like Eritrea and Sudan, who are looking for a new home and complain of the virulent racism that they encounter in Israel. However, the district has other aspects, best explored during the daytime, when the market is open.

The haTikva quarter was established in the 1930s for municipal workers, most of whom came from Arab countries. Until the 1980s, the residents here were almost entirely Jews from Yemen, Iran, Iraq and Egypt. In the 1990s, Jews of European origin also came to the quarter, as a result of a wave of immigration from the former Soviet Union.

If you walk through the alleys, some of them only just wide enough for a car to pass, you will see small single-storey houses, and some that are even tinier: two rooms with a roof above. To the south of the market lie a few streets with a noticeably large number of whitewashed buildings. They used to be known as the Salonika houses, as their original inhabitants came from Salonika in Greece and worked in the harbour of Tel Aviv. Like tens of thousands of other Jews, these people immigrated to Palestine in the 1930s – in time to avoid occupation by the Germans and deportation. Although the present-day haTikva quarter is home to a mixture of old-established residents and more recent arrivals from Africa, you can still plainly see the little white houses, especially in Roni Street, Kemuel Street and Azai Street, that once reminded the occupants of their Greek homeland.

**Address** Roni, Kemuel and Azai Street, Tel Aviv – haTikva | **Getting there** Bus 7, 16 or 204 to Etzel / Hanoch | **Tip** The market in the haTikva quarter is more extensive and pleasanter than Carmel Market. The range of goods is smaller, but the prices are significantly lower.

# 83 The Sarona Estate
*Redevelopment with dubious results*

In 1871, German Templers founded a colony about four kilometres north of Jaffa: Sarona. From Germany they had brought both agricultural equipment and practical know-how, so that they were successful at farming. They grew grapes for wine as well as citrus fruit, and were role models for Jewish immigrants in this work. During World War II the inhabitants of Sarona and other Templers from Palestine, who included many members of the Nazi party and persons with strong anti-Semitic views, were interned and ultimately deported. The buildings of Sarona were first used by the British army and Mandate government, and after 1948 were taken over by the Israeli army and government institutions.

Some of the Templer buildings today belong to the Kirya, the headquarters of the army, but the land to the south of Kaplan Street has been sold. For the 100th anniversary of Tel Aviv, at the heart of the city, an area where land is expensive, 18 buildings were restored there. They are now situated in a park, surrounded by high-rises, and their gabled roofs, so reminiscent of provincial German architecture, compete with the glass façades of the luxury apartments that encircle them.

It is hard to be overcome by pastoral feelings here. The fact that Sarona is in essence a shopping zone makes this impossible. However beautifully the buildings have been renovated, the city authorities have justifiably been criticised, as they are now occupied by design shops, stores selling sports items and restaurants. Yes, there is a visitor centre too, but its opening times are an enigma, and it only gives a highly superficial account of the history of the Templers. At weekends, guided tours are organised that re-enact the life of the Templers in deliberately comical scenes, played with a strong German accent. Today, Sarona is one of the less attractive sides of Tel Aviv, more illusion than reality.

**Address** Between Eliezer Kaplan and haArba'a Street, Tel Aviv – Sarona Gardens (Ganei Sarona) | **Getting there** Bus 63 to haShuk hasitoani / haHashmonaim, bus 239 to Kaplan / Aluf Mendler | **Tip** In the lobby of the three skyscrapers at the edge of the Sarona Park, a huge gourmet strip has opened under the name Sarona Market, based on big market halls in Spain and England. Almost 8,000 square metres are devoted to selling fruit, vegetables, fine foods and freshly made meals.

# 84 — The Shalom Aleichem House

*Ven du vilst redn yidish*

If you go south along Weizmann Street, passing the triangular Heart Center of the hospital to the new building for the law courts, in the side street, where there is another tall office tower, you can see a small stone building that does not fit at all in. The building is thus involuntarily a symbol for this place: Berkovich Street 2 is a centre for the Yiddish language and culture of Jews from Eastern Europe.

Founded in 1966 and named after Shalom Aleichem, the building accommodates a well-stocked library, the archive of the writer and a small permanent exhibition about his life and work. Born in 1859 near Kiev under the name Shalom Rabinovitz, he first started to write for Hebrew newspapers before deciding to publish his works in Yiddish, and thus became one of the fathers of the new Yiddish literature that blossomed in Eastern Europe in the late 19th century. His best-known characters include Tevye the Dairyman, Menachem Mendel and Motl Peyse dem Khazns. Shalom Aleichem died in 1916 in New York. The Shalom Aleichem House is also home to the archive of Yitzchak Dov Berkovich, Sholem Aleichem's son-in-law, who was his executor, translated his works into Hebrew, was a writer himself and played a major part in founding the Yiddish centre.

Every year some 300 people take part in courses in the Yiddish language and the culture of the Jews of Eastern Europe, according to Professor Avraham Novershtern, who is director of the centre. Among them are increasing numbers of young people who take an interest in the language, which was neglected in Israel for a long time. To be convinced that Yiddish is by no means old-fashioned, take a look at the Facebook page of the Shalom Aleichem House, where in addition to events listings all kinds of amusing contributions are gathered.

ניו שלום עליכם

Address Berkovich Street 2, Tel Aviv – New North, www.facebook.com/Beth.Shalom.
Aleichem | **Getting there** Bus 7, 18 or 59 to Beit haMischpat/Weizmann | **Hours**
Sun–Thu 10am–6pm | **Tip** Diagonally opposite at no. 4 Weizmann Street stands Beit
Asia. Built in 1979, it is known for its unique structure, which creates a play of light
and shade from the horizontal bands of the façade without any corners. Beit Asia
accommodates offices including the Swedish, Italian and Vietnamese embassies.

# 85 __ The Shalom Meir Tower

*An exhibition with the concrete charm of the 1960s*

It is the worst eyesore in Tel Aviv, and looks no better even if you know that it was once the tallest building in the Middle East: the Shalom Meir Tower, completed in 1965. This skyscraper occupied the site of what had been the Herzliya School at the end of Herzl Street. A unique historic building was thus destroyed once and for all. The school was founded in 1905 in Jaffa and moved to Herzl Street in 1909. In the 1960s it was not thought important to keep this impressive work of architecture, which combined Modern International and specifically Eretz Israeli elements.

The 34-storey tower undoubtedly took a prominent place in the cityscape. It used to accommodate many government departments, for example the local branch of the Interior Ministry and the citizens' registry office, a small department store called Kolbo Shalom, a waxworks museum and of course lots of offices. In the end, criticism of the demolition of the school was voiced and led to the establishment of a committee to protect the city heritage.

A small consolation for the loss is that an exhibition on the history of Tel Aviv has been installed in the lobby and on the first floor of the Shalom Meir Tower. The displays are a little dated, but worth seeing nevertheless. Photographs, maps and models chart the development of the city, especially of the first residential district, Ahuzat Bait. Hundreds of photographs show the city in later years, its cultural and social life, Tel Aviv's Bauhaus architecture and coffee houses, and the school, Gymnasia Herzliya. A special exhibition is dedicated to Arie Akiva Weiss, the initiator and former chairman of Ahuzat Bait. The walls of the lobby are adorned by a 100-square-metre mosaic by Nahum Gutman and a second, smaller mosaic by David Sharir. The collection of ceramics that were fashionable in the 1920s is also wonderful.

מגדל שלום מאיר

**Address** Achad haAm Street 9, Tel Aviv – City Centre | **Getting there** Bus 18, 22, 38, 61 or 82 to Migdal Shalom/Ahad haAm | **Hours** Sun–Thu 8am–7pm, Fri 8am–2pm, free admission | **Tip** The house in which Arie Akiva Weiss lived fortunately still stands, on the corner at no. 2 Herzl Street. One of the most attractive houses in Ahuzat Bait, planned by Weiss himself, it was built in 1909, originally single-storey, and then extended upwards. Today it has been restored and is in its original condition.

# 86 _ Sheinkin

*The decline of a street?*

Sheinkin Street, which became a symbol of Tel Aviv as a hip bubble in the late 1980s, long ago ceased to be what it once was. The avant-garde street scene of those days has largely given way to the usual fashion boutiques and cafés, and the facelift that the city authorities gave the street makes everything seem much more orderly. Moreover, the redevelopment has driven out many shops, and Sheinkin, once famous for its artistic subculture, now exudes the air of a perfectly normal side street in the evenings. Its old icons have gone, and those who are looking for the atmosphere of the old days moved on to the south of the city long ago.

In June 2015 the legendary Café Tamar closed its doors after 60 years. It was once the main rendezvous for left-wing intellectuals and a place for critical debate on politics and society. These glory days may be a distant memory, but journalists, artists, writers and composers were still to be found among the loyal customers of the owner, Sarah Stern, who died at the age of 90 only a few months after the café closed. In March 2018 the street said goodbye to a further icon, Orna and Ella. The restaurant run by Ella Shine and Orna Agmon kept going here for a good 25 years thanks to its highly distinctive mix of good food and a pleasantly relaxed yet high-class atmosphere. Diners who came here will never forget the levivot batata, fritters made from sweet potatoes, that Orna and Ella served. Here too, renovation of the building was the occasion for the two owners to take their leave, after the street was, in their words, 'badly abused'.

In this case it is entirely justifiable to mourn the passing of the good old days. On the other hand, the renovation work has made the architectural gems of the street resplendent once again, and Sheinkin Street is still a pleasant place to take a stroll.

Address Sheinkin Street, Tel Aviv – City Centre | Getting there Bus 23 to Sheinkin/Johanan haSandlar, in the opposite direction to Beit haSefer Balfour, bus 5 or 142 to Sderot Rothschild/Sheinkin | Tip In the Sheinkin Garden is the Beit Tami community centre. Alongside various weekly courses for children and adults from sports, art and languages to cookery and robotics, public events, readings and exhibitions often take place there.

# 87 — The Shelanu Supermarket
*A social cooperative with big aims*

In summer 2014, the debate about food prices in Tel Aviv heated up, not for the first time, when a Facebook user compared them with prices in Berlin. But there was no sign of mass demonstrations, as there had been three years earlier, and most Israelis place themselves without protest in the clutches of the major supermarket chains. This contrasts with the attitude of a group of committed Tel Aviv citizens who got together during the protests of 2011 and decided to do something. An initial result of this can be visited in the Bitzaron district.

The group founded a cooperative called Shelanu ('Ours'). Its members, who numbered 470 in early 2015, are both the owners and customers, and work on the project as unpaid volunteers. The first project is a small supermarket. You don't see a big difference in prices, even if many items are a few shekels cheaper here. But this shop with a surface of 160 square metres cannot compete with the big chains, of course. The purpose is rather to establish conscious, sustainable shopping according to the principles of the cooperative: fair, transparent, with equality and social justice. Shelanu's aim is to pave the way for a social and economic transformation that will ultimately also reduce the cost of living.

These principles are proclaimed on yellow signs on the shelves of the shop. There is no decoration here, no big advertisements, but instead a high-class assortment. Organic products are sold alongside 'normal' ones, wholemeal pasta sharing a shelf with noodles made from refined flour. You don't have to search high and low to find the organic ketchup. Shelanu stocks its displays with what the customers, that is the owners, want to buy.

The plan is that this supermarket will be only the beginning of the project. Shelanu is now working to establish a cooperative bank, as well as a cooperative pension and social security fund.

Address Sderot haHaskala 9, Tel Aviv – Bitzaron | Getting there Bus 23 or 279 to
Derech haShalom / Tozeret haAretz, bus 7, 54 or 239 to Yigal Alon / Derech haShalom |
Hours Sun – Thu 7am – 9pm, Fri 7am – 3pm | Tip Just round the corner at no. 14
Kremitski Street is Café Lachmanina. Following some uproar about the personal
biography of the transgender proprietor, Lachmanina has proved its worth thanks
to its bread, cake and other treats.

# 88　Shfela Street

*How did the Washington palm get to Tel Aviv?*

If you turn from busy, three-lane Derech Menachem Begin into haShfela Street, you see them straight away: four slender palm trees as big as houses that you would expect to find in California rather than in this modest street, only 60 metres long. In fact, they are Mexican Washington palms (*Washingtonia robusta*), which here seem out of place. They are the last remaining witnesses to the long-gone golden age of this little street, which now seems very run-down. The palms, originally five in number, were planted in 1927. They flanked the approach to the city's new trade-fair grounds. The Washington palm was not new in Palestine, as it had been planted as early as 1890, first of all in Sarona and Neve Tzedek. They are easy to maintain and elegant, exactly the right style for the access road to the new trade-fair site. After two fairs had successfully been held in 1924 in school buildings in Achad haAm Street, the search began for a larger site. Land belonging to an insurance company with an area of 15,000 square metres was leased and a large exhibition hall constructed there. On 25 October, 1925 the first fair opened, with 330 exhibitors. In contrast to previous events, at which mainly goods of Jewish production from Palestine were shown, this one was an international show. There were 121 exhibitors from abroad who took part, including some from neighbouring Arab countries. Big companies such as Singer, General Motors, Renault and Shell also presented their products here.

Up to 1932, four more international trade fairs took place here. At the same time the venue was used for big events and open-air concerts, and had its own funfair. By the early 1930s this site too had become too small, and the trade fair moved to the mouth of the river Yarkon. Nothing more can be seen of the old trade-fair site, as the exhibition hall was demolished in 1995.

**Address** haShfela Street, Tel Aviv – Neve Sha'anan | **Getting there** Bus 1, 5, 40, 42 or 89 to Hevrat haHashmal / Derech Begin | **Tip** At the junction of Derech Begin Street and haRakevet Street stands Beit Hadar with its characteristic round façade. Constructed between 1936 and 1938, it was not only the city's first building with a steel structure but also the first office building.

# 89 __ The Ship Building

*A flagship of the International Modern style*

Its proper name is Beit Shimon Levi, but the striking building at the busy junction of haMasger Street, haRakevet Street and Levanda Street is better known as Beit haOnia (the Ship Building). Erected in 1934–35, it is one of the best-known examples of the International Modern style, which is so dominant in Tel Aviv, but its location far from the architectural treasures of the city centre means that it gets few visitors.

Yet this building in Levanda Street, along which the railway to Jaffa once passed, is extremely special, partly because of its location. Shimon Hamadi Levi, who owned the site, is said to have planned the Ship Building himself and to have constructed it with his own hands. In doing so he boldly disregarded the existing regulations, which stipulated that nothing was to have more than three storeys, by building it with a cellar, ground floor, three upper storeys and a small attic with additional rooms, i.e. a total of six floors. The building narrows towards the crossroads like a triangle with an acute angle, and thanks to its impressive height resembles a ship.

After a lengthy conflict, an agreement was reached between Levi and Mayor Dizengoff, and so the Ship Building remained the tallest structure in the area for many years.

By 1937, the Levi family themselves had had to leave it, for financial reasons. Since that time the building has been home to a synagogue and also served as an observation point for the Hagana, one of the military organisations that operated before the state of Israel was founded. It is still used for residential purposes. Although it has the status of protected heritage and was renovated in 1990 and 2007, it looks a little shabby and has also been disfigured by a mast for mobile telephony. Next door a 25-storey tower will soon be built that will overshadow the Ship Building once and for all.

**Address** Levanda Street 56, Tel Aviv – Neve Sha'anan | **Getting there** Bus 51 or 60 to haMasger/Yad Charutzim, in the opposite direction to haMasger/La Guardia, or a 10-minute walk along Rosh Pina Street from the central bus station | **Tip** In Rosh Pina Street, which also ends at the corner where Beit haOnia is located, stand two further beautiful though unrestored buildings in the Bauhaus style, no. 26 and no. 28. House no. 26, also dating from 1935 but built in a horseshoe shape, looks slightly like the chubby little brother of Beit haOnia.

# 90___Shuk Shuka

*When a longing for shakshuka takes hold*

Of course, there are many places in Tel Aviv, and especially in Jaffa, where you can get a really good shakshuka. But the best surroundings for a good, fresh shakshuka are found at the market, as this dish depends on fresh ingredients that are only to be had at the market, and it is also a simple meal that is wonderful as a snack eaten while shopping. Shakshuka is poached eggs in a thick sauce made from tomatoes (of which Israel can boast some of the finest in the world), onions, peppers and other vegetables as desired, for example spinach, served in a small baking form or pan. You eat the meal with bread or pitta, which is used to mop up the sauce.

At Shuk Shuka – the name is a play on words, as Shuk means market – in a small side street just a few paces from the market, they serve alongside the classic dish and an extra-spicy version an Italian one with basil and goat's cheese, a Spanish one with chickpeas, spinach and salami, and a Greek shakshuka with grilled vegetables and feta cheese. There are also various small dishes, like Spanish tapas or Greek snacks, but made with an Israeli twist. When all of this is washed down with beer, ouzo and arak lemonade, the customers are in a good mood.

The charm of this place, which is a little bit like the essence of the atmosphere of the city as a whole, is the simple but refined ambience. You sit on stools at a bar clad with African tiles and have a direct view of the modest kitchen. The aromas that waft over, good music and pleasant company make it a perfect shakshuka experience. If you like things to be quiet, it is best to come in the morning for an espresso and some breakfast. If, on the other hand, you want to see the place buzzing, Friday is the right day. Then a second row of stools is put out, and the atmosphere matches the Greek music that animates you to start enjoying the weekend.

**Address** Simtat haCarmel 30, Tel Aviv – Kerem haTeimanim | **Getting there** Bus 10, 24, 61, 63 or 66 and others to Carmelite | **Hours** Sun – Thu 9am – 6pm, Fri 8am – 3pm or 4pm | **Tip** There used to be two kinds of cheese in Israel: white and yellow. Those days are long gone, but if you are looking for truly excellent cheeses, you have to go to Davka Gourmet at the market, right opposite the street Simtat haCarmel.

# 91 Simta Plonit

*How did the lion come to a dead end?*

The 'anonymous alley' and the 'unknown alley' live up to their names. For many years these two parallel dead-end streets, which run off from King George Street, were a cultural hotspot with galleries and cafés. Those days are over, even though new shops or cafés try their luck in the alleys from time to time. Nevertheless, it is always pleasant to come here, especially to the 'unknown' one, Simta Plonit, at the end of which is a statue of a lion.

When you enter from noisy, busy King George Street, it feels a bit like being suddenly immersed in a different era. This narrow street may not be closed to traffic, but there is little point in driving there, and so it is pleasantly quiet. Most of the buildings have now been renovated. The nicest of them is number 7, of course, at the end of the alley. Meir Getzel Shapiro, a rich American Jew from Detroit, built it in 1922. He had moved to Palestine, bought land and invested. The Shapira district in the south of the city is named after him. In the centre of Tel Aviv he built a house in the eclectic style as a place where his wife Sonya would feel at home. The statue of a lion was a present for her.

However, all of Shapiro's money was clearly not enough to fulfil his wish of having the two dead-end alleys named after himself and his wife. Mayor Dizengoff succeeded in preventing this. Pending an agreement, the two alleys were given the names 'anonymous' and 'unknown'. No solution to the conflict was found, and so they have kept their names to this day. For many years the lion was in a decayed condition and started to crumble.

Recently the statue was restored by the city authorities and given a coat of white paint. The lion, by the way, is depicted on the cover of Arik Einstein's and Joni Rechter's famous record *I Was Once a Child*, on which 'Adon Shoko' and 'Shabat baBoker' are commemorated.

**Address** Simta Plonit 7, Tel Aviv – City Centre | **Getting there** Bus 18, 25, 61 or 72 to haMelech George / Rashi, in the opposite direction to haMelech George / haHashmonaim | **Tip** The Little Prince, a café with a second-hand bookshop, used to be in Simta Plonit. Today it is not far away, at the corner of King George Street 19. You can enjoy its living-room atmosphere over a cup of coffee or in the evening at a book launch or other events.

# 92 — The Special Beaches
*Different ways of having fun by the sea*

The people of Tel Aviv love dogs, especially large ones, which are a prominent feature of the city – even though, in view of the small size of homes here, that may not seem logical. There are 20,000 dogs registered in the city, but the real figure must be many times higher. You certainly get this impression from the frequent fouling of the pavements, which turn a walk through the streets into an obstacle course, in spite of the draconian punishments imposed on those who don't pick it up. Many people keep dogs such as huskies and St Bernards that are not suited to the city's climate. For some, the dog is only a status symbol, but most dog owners look after their four-legged friends. People who have to work long hours hire a dog sitter.

Around the city there are 60 dog playgrounds, in small parks, in Yarkon Park and on the boulevards, where they can be let off the lead, which is normally not allowed. In the north of the city a section of beach has even been designated for dogs. This strip of sand beneath Independence Park (see ch. 51) may be relatively small, but it enables dog owners to sunbathe while their pets run around, play and go into the water. Swimming is an all-year-round activity on the dog beach, so even in bad weather you can watch the pets having a good time in the water and frolicking about.

In general there seems to be a preference for dividing the beach up into allocated sections. Indeed, extremely diverse special beaches border on each other: in the south is Tel Aviv's gay beach, called Hilton Beach, which is the place to be in the scene in summer and especially during Gay Pride Week. Adjoining it to the north is the 'orthodox' beach, where men and women are admitted separately on different days and can enjoy a somewhat quieter strip of sand without being exposed to the possible nuisance of approaches by members of the opposite sex.

Address Shlomo Lahat Promenade, beneath Gan haAtzmaut, Tel Aviv – Old North | Getting there Bus 4, 9 or 13 to Ben Yehuda/Jabotinsky | Tip On Fridays between noon and 4pm animal welfare organisations offer dogs for adoption in King George Street, by the fence of Gan Meir. This is the other aspect of loving dogs – nice to see and sad at the same time.

# 93__ Sportek
*Mastering the Yemeni step*

From the grounds of Sportek, a place used for games of basketball and work-outs for the muscles, Shabbat music wafts through Yarkon Park. From 11 o'clock in the morning, anyone can come here to dance and show their skill at 'rikudei am', Israeli folk dances. The people who do this in the park on the morning of Shabbat are a group of regulars, but anyone can come along and join in – young and old, couples, singles and families. The dancing goes on for three hours, in a big circle, alone and in pairs. It doesn't take long before newcomers can keep up with the others in the basic step.

Israeli folk dancing developed in the 1940s. The hour of its birth is said to have been a celebration of Shavuot in the Dalia kibbutz in 1944. The first festival of folk dance was held in the same year. From the beginning, 'rikudei am' were more than just entertainment. They helped to mould an emerging nation, as they united influences from various countries of origin of Eastern European Jews, especially the hora from Romania and traditional Russian dances, to form a distinct Eretz Israeli style. Since the 1980s, folk dance has been popular in large parts of the population, including city dwellers. An estimated 300,000 Israelis regularly participate in folk dancing. Thousands of choreographed dances have now been documented, and new ones are added every year. On Shabbat, there are opportunities to dance for free all over the country. In Tel Aviv, another place for this is Gordon Beach.

Here in the park the atmosphere is different – more intimate and sociable, and the place is greener, of course. Four teachers alternate so that different styles are practised together. On a hill next to the asphalted dance floor you can sit on the grass and watch – and, if you are new to it, you might then dare to join in. Don't worry, you will soon master the Yemeni step.

Address Yarkon Park, north bank, halfway between Ibn Gvirol Street and Derech Namir, Tel Aviv – Yarkon Park | **Getting there** Bus 12, 13, 189 or 289 to Sportek/Sderot Rokach | **Hours** Summer 11am–7pm | **Tip** Further west beyond Ibn Gvirol Street lies Gan haBanim, a place of memorial for victims of war and terror from Tel Aviv. Eleven different groves symbolise wars and times of unrest and violence. The names of the fallen are inscribed on slabs of black granite.

# 94 The Street Libraries

*Summer reading for passers-by*

What could be pleasanter than relaxing in a deckchair and leafing through a book? It is very easy to do this in Tel Aviv in summer, and you don't have to carry your own lounger around with you. In cooperation with Beit Ariela (see ch. 11), the city government has introduced a wonderful project: mobile street libraries, which are now scattered across the city in 11 locations.

In fact, they are small trailers that stand on a patch of grass. Every day between 8 o'clock in the morning and 8 o'clock in the evening, the hatches at the side are opened and a small library appears. Each of these trailers holds about 500 books in all kinds of different languages, including Hebrew, Arabic, Russian, English and French. They are continually restocked and added to. Of course, some books don't come back, but to make up for this there are people who donate books instead of stealing them. There is certainly plenty to browse through: novels, children's books, magazines, something for everyone. This is not about finding the latest bestseller. Instead the idea is to discover a book to enjoy amongst all the others. And if you don't want to read, you will at least be pleased with the comfortable loungers.

The street libraries are deliberately not only positioned in parks but on small green spaces where people pass by. One of them is at the end of Rothschild Boulevard with a view of haBima Square (see ch. 41), another in Bitzaron on the newly created green area of haHaskala Boulevard. The point of the project is to encourage people to pause for thought for a short moment, something that is undoubtedly needed in a noisy city like Tel Aviv. When you lie back on a lounger with a book, for a minute or two you can shut out all the hectic activity around you. The mobile libraries are set up from May to November. That is more or less how long summer lasts in Tel Aviv.

Address For example at Sderot Rothschild /Kikar haBima or Sderot haHaskala, Tel Aviv – City Centre or Tel Aviv – Bitzaron | Getting there Bus 5 to haBima/Sderot Rothschild, bus 39 or 63 to haBima/Sderot Ben Zion or bus 23 or 279 to Derech haShalom/Tozeret haAretz | Tip Mobile libraries are also available in summer at Gordon Beach and Metzitzim Beach, with more literature in English, which suits the surroundings.

# 95 __ Sumeil

*Last memories of an Arab village*

Tel Aviv was built on sand dunes. The first Hebrew city of modern times arose here from nothing. That, at least, is the legend as it is usually told. This version is in need of a little correction, as there were several Arab villages, for example Sumeil, in the area now covered by the city. The remains of this village, which once stood on a hill and was surrounded by plantations and farmland, can today be found on one of the main roads in Tel Aviv.

In the early 1930s, Sumeil had 650 inhabitants. Later, a few Jewish families lived here, renting rooms on the lower floors of the small houses. Whereas relations between the two ethnic groups were still intact in those days, at least to the extent that the children could play together, the situation came to a head in 1947. When the United Nations plan for partitioning the country became known, the Arab residents of Sumeil fled, fearing escalation. They were not to return, as the War of Independence broke out after the foundation of the state of Israel.

Since then, the houses of the village have been occupied by Jews, many of them new arrivals from Arab states. The city and national governments simply ignored these circumstances. No eviction orders were issued until the 1960s – not because this was Arab property, but because some of the houses stood in the way of a widening of the street. In the end, they were evacuated forcibly and torn down. Today only a small part of the village remains. The last of the houses will probably disappear in the foreseeable future, as the land is too valuable for building. Negotiations with the remaining families have been going on for many years, while plans for stylish high-rises are at the ready.

You still can – and definitely should! – take a look at what remains of the Arab village of Sumeil, because this too is part of the history of the city of Tel Aviv.

**Address** Corner of Ibn Gvirol and Arlozorov Street, Tel Aviv – New North | **Getting there** Bus 24, 25 or 189 to Ibn Gvirol / Arlozorov | **Tip** At the north-eastern edge of the large car park behind the houses of Sumeil lies the Hechal Yehuda synagogue, built in the 1970s in the shape of a shell. It is used mainly by Jews from Salonika and observes Sephardic rites (entrance from Ben Saruk Street).

# 96  The Suzanne Dellal Centre
*Paper boats in the courtyard*

In the middle of Neve Tzedek lies one of the most important and best-loved cultural institutions in Israel, the Suzanne Dellal Centre for modern dance and drama. Three stages are devoted to performances by Israeli choreographers and ensembles and international guests. The centre is home to the Batsheva Dance Company, the Inbal Dance Company and the Orna Porat Theatre for children and young people. The special charm of this institution lies not only in the excellence of the productions but also in the combination of a historic site with modern use. The various buildings of the centre were originally part of a school founded in the 1890s by Jewish relief organisations. In those days girls and boys were taught separately here. Later, until the 1970s, the classes were mixed. A further building accommodated the Levinsky Teacher Training College. Renovation of the site was made possible with assistance from the Dellal family from London, in memory of their daughter, and lasted five years. When the Suzanne Dellal Centre was opened in 1989, it gave an impetus to the gentrification of the district, which became so shabby in the 1960s that the city government planned to demolish it.

Today this is unimaginable: Neve Tzedek has now been largely restored, and the streets are full of cafés, restaurants and unusual shops. The Suzanne Dellal Centre is at the heart of the quarter. Its large courtyards are wonderful spots for sitting and resting if you have not come to see a performance. They were designed by the landscape architect Shlomo Aronson and received the prestigious Schechter Prize. Whereas the south courtyard has lawns and palm trees, the large courtyard has been sparingly planted. Small water channels, connected to each other underground, flow around citrus trees, so that you can have a great time playing with little paper boats.

**Address** Yehieli Street 5, Tel Aviv – Neve Tzedek, www.suzannedellal.org.il | Getting there Bus 10, 11, 18 or 37 to Prof Kaufmann/Shenkar, from there via Shenkar and Shlush Street in about 10 minutes to the Suzanne Dellal Centre | Hours Accessible 24 hours | Tip The Suzanne Dellal Centre is a good starting point for exploring the quarter with its picturesque little streets. Heading north-east on Shabazi Street you will see many of the shops and cafés typical of Neve Tzedek.

# 97 __ The Tel Aviv Greeters

*Explore the city with friends*

In Tel Aviv there are at least as many guided tours as facets of the city. Conventional historical tours, Bauhaus tours, walks through various districts, around the markets, or in search of graffiti – there is something for every taste. If you want a special experience, you can contact the Tel Aviv greeters. They are part of a worldwide network, and here, as in New York and Chicago, Paris and London, Berlin and Rome, they make it possible to book a guided tour of the city as if you were meeting friends. The principle behind the greeter network is that residents present their city free of charge, motivated entirely by enthusiasm for their home town.

This is a brilliant idea, as it enables visitors to get to know the city from a completely different angle, to hear stories from the neighbourhood and meet people on the spot. Even though it is not difficult to strike up a conversation in Tel Aviv, a greeter tour is a great way to get close to the city and its inhabitants.

The service is free of charge, but a firm booking is expected. Three weeks in advance you make the arrangements, giving exact details about yourself and where you are staying. Laila, the extremely nice coordinator, makes efforts to match people together according to their age and interests. There is a big choice of greeters.

Doron, for example, likes to meet his visitors on Fridays to stroll with them along Rothschild Boulevard and across Levinsky Market, then through Neve Tzedek or to Tachana (see ch. 35), where he takes them to his favourite café. On Fridays, says Doron, Tel Aviv has a special atmosphere that he has not encountered anywhere else in the world. Along the way he explains how the city is changing, points out hidden cafés, lets his visitors sniff at spices and nuts, and buys them a malabi. It is like taking a walk with friends to kick off the weekend.

Address www.telavivgreeter.com | Tip For other tours see, for example, the official tourist website of the city: www.visit-tel-aviv.com.

# 98__ The Tel Aviv Museum

*A modern building with the world's most beautiful restaurant*

In 2011, the Tel Aviv Museum of Art inaugurated its extension: the Herta and Paul Amir Building. A connecting structure on the edge of the sculpture garden links it to the older building, which has occupied a site on Shaul haMelech Boulevard between the Beit Ariela municipal library (see ch. 11) and the law courts since 1971. The museum houses the most important collection of Israeli art and an impressive cross-section of international art from the 19th century to the present day, including works by Chagall, Kandinsky and Picasso.

The extension was designed by the architect Preston Scott Cohen, who teaches at the Harvard Graduate School of Design. Its five levels, on which the exhibition spaces are interwoven, are connected by the brightly lit, spiral atrium that Preston describes as a 'lightfall'. The opening in 2011 featured, among other exhibitions, a large retrospective of the work of Anselm Kiefer. The new building also accommodates the Gallery of German Friends, which opened with a collection of graphic works by German Expressionist artists and is used for temporary exhibitions with a German cultural background.

When you have been round the museum and are in need of a break, you can recover in the world's most beautiful restaurant: the Pastel Brasserie in the new museum extension. In 2014 it won the International Space Design Award – Idea Tops. The design by Alon Baranowitz and Irene Kronenberg, in dark colours, blends harmoniously with the architecture of the building. The Pastel Brasserie follows a trend in big museums away from basic cafeterias to stylish restaurants that are also open to customers who are not visiting the museum. Award or no award, the brasserie is undoubtedly a nice place for mulling over what you have seen in the exhibitions while enjoying a snack or a proper meal.

HERTA & PAUL AMIR BUILDING

TEL AVIV MUSEUM OF ART מוזיאון תל אביב לאמנות

הבניין ע"ש שמואל והרטה עמיר

**Address** Shaul haMelech Boulevard 27, Tel Aviv – New North | Getting there
Bus 9, 38 or 82 to Beit haMischpat / Sderot Shaul haMelech | Hours Mon, Wed & Sat
10am – 6pm, Tue & Thu 10am – 9pm, Fri 10am – 2pm | Tip Another part of the
Tel Aviv Museum of Art is the Helena Rubinstein Pavilion for Contemporary Art
on Kikar haBimah, which is devoted to temporary exhibitions of contemporary art in
diverse styles.

# 99___ The Traffic Island
### *A grand stage on King Albert Square*

The two benches have the finest view if you are interested in architecture. The small square named after King Albert I of Belgium at the heart of the city has a traffic island at its centre, just big enough for two massive fig trees and two benches. It has to be admitted that the traffic spoils the pleasure on weekdays. The best time to sit here is Friday afternoon, when the light becomes soft and peace descends on the city. Then you can examine at leisure the buildings that surround the square. To the west is the striking Beit haPagoda, built in 1925 for the American Morris Bloch. It was designed by the architect Alexander Levy (see ch. 101), and the pagoda structures that Bloch liked were added around the balconies, which are essential in the hot climate of Tel Aviv. Bloch occupied the house himself, while the upper storey was the residence of the Polish consul, for whom a lift was specially built. After Bloch's death, small businesses arrived: flowers were sold in the courtyard, doctors had their surgeries there, and a small synagogue moved in too. Over the years, the building fell into decay, and has been used for residential purposes again only since a lengthy restoration that was carried out in the 1990s.

On the south side a building by Dov Karmi, one of the leading Bauhaus architects in Israel, has undergone an interesting transformation: the interior was gutted and the architect's son, Ram Karmi, designed a postmodern structure at the back. The façade has also been covered by a work of the artist Uri Lifshitz, a pattern in metal that corresponds to the trees in the middle of the square and the shadows that they cast.

The other buildings in eclectic styles around the square have all now been restored, now giving onlookers the impression that they might be abroad, perhaps sitting on a bench in a quiet corner of Paris.

**Address** Kikar haMelech Albert, at the junction of Nachmani, Montefiori and Bezalel Yafe Street, Tel Aviv – City Centre | **Getting there** Bus 5 or 142 to Sderot Rothschild/Nachmani or Sderot Rothschild/haBursa | **Tip** Brioche and café au lait in Café Ben Ami at the north-east corner of the square help to enhance the Paris feeling. All the cakes and quiches can be recommended.

# 100_ Trumpeldor Cemetery
*A stroll through the politics and culture of the Yishuv*

Trumpeldor Cemetery was laid out in 1902, when a cholera epidemic was raging in Jaffa and the Ottoman government banned burials in the old Jewish cemetery (see ch. 73). At that time, seven years before the city of Tel Aviv was founded, Shimon Rokach (see ch. 80), one of the founders of Neve Tzedek, received from the government a piece of land well to the north of the area that was then populated, so that he could establish a cemetery there.

When you walk through the gate in narrow, single-lane Trumpeldor Street, first you pass the mass graves in which were buried the victims of the Arab unrest of 1921, including the writer Josef Chaim Brenner, and of those killed in 1929 and in the Arab revolt between 1936 and 1939. In the eastern part of the labyrinthine, hilly site are the oldest of the approximately 5,000 graves. The prominent people, by contrast, are in the south-west. Until 1932 this was the only cemetery in the city in which you could find the who's who of the Yishuv. It is the burial ground for founders of the city such as Shimon Rokach, Aharon Shlush and Menachem Sheinkin, for politicians, first and foremost Mayor Meir Dizengoff, and for Zionists such as Max Nordau, Ahad haAm and Chaim Arlozorov. The Hebrew national poet Chaim Nachman Bialik was laid to rest here, as was the author Ephraim Kishon.

For many years now there have been hardly any free spaces for new burials, and those that remain are sold at very high prices. The grave of the Yemeni singer Shoshana Damari is said to have cost a quarter of a million shekels in 2006. One of the last 'newcomers' is also a musician, Arik Einstein, who died in November 2013. The music of this singer and actor could be described as the soundtrack to the history of the country. His grave is at the south-west end of the cemetery, near the boundary wall. The reddish gravestone can be plainly seen from a distance.

**Address** Trumpeldor Street 19, Tel Aviv – City Centre | **Getting there** Bus 22 or
66 to Trumpeldor/Pinsker, in the opposite direction to Bograshov/Pinsker | **Hours**
Summer Sun–Thu 6.30am–7pm, Fri 6.30am–2pm, winter Sun–Thu 6.30am–5pm,
Fri 6.30am–2pm | **Tip** Arik Einstein lived close to his last resting place at no. 40 Chovevei
Zion Street. The memorial in front of the house is a grey rock with a broken guitar and
the words of his famous song Ani ve-ata: *Me and You.*

# 101 Ussishkin's House

*In memory of an almost forgotten architect*

The German-Jewish architect Alexander Levy, born in 1883, had a leading role in a successful Berlin architectural practice after completing his studies. Levy, a committed Zionist in his early years, emigrated to Palestine, where he opened a small office in Tel Aviv, in 1920. One of the wonderful buildings in the eclectic style that he designed in those years stands at the corner of haYarkon Street and Allenby Street. It was built in 1922 for Menachem Ussishkin, a Zionist leader after whom it is named, although he only lived in it for a very short time. Beautiful details such as the tall pointed arches and the stone-decorated lunette are only revealed when you stand right in front of the house and take time to walk around it.

Alexander Levy did not stay long in Palestine. Lack of commissions and the difficulties of adapting to the country led him to return to Berlin in 1927. In 1932, concerned at political developments, he moved to Paris. Levy was deported to Auschwitz in August 1942 and murdered there. The house in Tel Aviv remained the property of the Ussishkin family until the 1990s and then, by now in a pitiful condition, was sold to a group of investors. On the condition that the original façade was retained, the city authorities gave approval for renovation, in the course of which two additional storeys, flanked with glass frontage, were added. From Ussishkin's house, looking towards the sea, you have a view of a small square, adorned by a fountain. On this spot, now the site of the Opera Tower, stood the Kessem cinema in the 1940s. The first sessions of the Knesset, the Israeli parliament, were held there in 1949, before the Knesset moved to Jerusalem in December. After that the Israeli Opera occupied the building until 1982. The square has changed its name repeatedly. Most people call it Opera Square, but its proper name is Knesset Square.

**Address** haYarkon Street 52, Tel Aviv – City Centre | Getting there Bus 13, 16, 17, 31, 63 or 66 to haYarkon / Allenby, in the opposite direction to Allenby / haKovshim | Tip A few houses further up, at no. 11 Allenby Street, stands another impressive building by Alexander Levy, with the nickname Admiralty House. It was restored to its former splendour in 2014.

# 102 The Voice of Peace

*Abie Nathan and his legendary pirate radio station*

'From somewhere in the Mediterranean, we are "The Voice of Peace".' This jingle is still well known, even though the pirate radio station that made it famous ceased to exist long ago. And the founder of Kol haShalom, the Voice of Peace, has now also passed away.

Abie Nathan, born in 1927 in Iran, was a pilot in the British Royal Air Force and fought in the Israeli War of Independence. He later worked as a pilot for El Al and opened a popular restaurant in Tel Aviv. In 1965 he stood for election to the Knesset (parliament), but did not get enough votes. Nevertheless, he tried to keep his promise to deliver a message of peace to Egypt, flying to Port Said on 28 February, 1966 in a biplane used for training pilots. Nathan was not able to hand over his message, but was arrested and sent back to Israel, but the legendary flight made him a hero of the peace movement.

In search of other ways to campaign for peace, in 1973 he founded a pirate radio station that broadcast 24 hours a day for 20 years from a ship that was anchored off the coast, five kilometres from Tel Aviv. The Voice of Peace was the first commercial radio station in Israel. DJs brought in from England played the hippest music on the ship. This was music that had never been heard before from an Israeli broadcaster and became extremely popular, especially with a young audience. The hopes aroused by the Oslo peace process of 1993 brought about Abie Nathan's decision to close down his radio station. He scuppered the ship and turned his attention to other humanitarian projects.

On Gordon Beach, a small commemorative plaque keeps alive the memory of this enterprise. Next to it is a loudspeaker. If you press the button, it plays the well-known jingles, gives a brief summary of the story of the Voice of Peace, and also plays a recording of Abie Nathan himself speaking a few words.

The Voice of Peace – קול השלום
1993 – 1973

5 km off this shore
Abie Nathan's peace ship was
anchored broadcasting messages
of peace, love and understanding

# 103 Washington Boulevard

*Tel Aviv's smallest boulevard in Florentin*

Of all names it could have, the smallest boulevard in Tel Aviv is called Washington, after the first president of the USA. Washington Boulevard ('Sderot Washington' in Hebrew) is all of 150 metres long and runs between Salame Street and Florentin Street. In Florentin, once a working-class district, these 150 metres of open space are a real treasure. On weekdays Florentin bursts at the seams. The small lanes with their artisan workshops and stores are always a scene of bustling activity, and cars crawl through it all in a desperate search for a parking space. One side of the boulevard was used for parking until a few years ago, but then remodelled and converted to a pedestrian zone. Now there are lots of places to sit beneath the big old fig trees. The 150 metres of boulevard display a bizarre mix of old and new. Next to an upholsterer that has been established for decades, you can find an alternative-style vegetarian shawarma snack bar, between a hip café and an art gallery a small synagogue that was recently restored.

At the end of the boulevard, at the corner of Florentin Street, a legendary bakery called Saloniki sold traditional Greek bread and cakes for 40 years. In the end, it had to make way for a new building. What has remained on the same corner is Bugsy – a cosy café by day and a trendy bar in the evening with live DJs. Bugsy has been going for 11 years, and used to be the only decent pub in the district. It long ago became an institution, not least because of its delicious food. And the French fries at Bugsy show for once why the Hebrew word for them is 'chips'.

By the way, no one knows any more why this boulevard was named after George Washington. On all sides it is surrounded by streets named after Zionists, which means that in terms of nomenclature, too, the street is a little island in the Florentin quarter.

**Address** Sderot Washington, between Derech Salame and Florentin Street,
Tel Aviv – Florentin | **Getting there** Bus 1, 25, 42 or 83 to Derech Salame / Ben Atar,
in the opposite direction to Derech Salame / Abulafia | **Tip** The Lehi Museum at no. 8
Avraham Stern Street, the continuation of Washington Boulevard, is devoted to the
history of the Lehi, a right-wing paramilitary organisation whose founder, Stern, was
shot by British police in this house in February 1942.

# 104_ The White City Centre

*German-Israeli cooperation in the Max Liebling House*

It is the world's biggest concentration of modernist buildings: 4,000 of them in the International Modern style make up Tel Aviv's so-called 'White City'. Its architects were all trained in Europe and brought the principles of their famous teachers to Palestine. For the young, rapidly growing city this style, often known for short as Bauhaus architecture, was just right: modern but plain, functional and without adornment.

The remarkable character of this architectural heritage was recognised officially when it was declared a UNESCO World Heritage site in 2003. To maintain it is, however, a major task to which the city is not really equal – not only because in the past there was a lack of awareness of the need to preserve monuments in Tel Aviv and there is a housing shortage, but also because the local climate means that the elements erode the buildings, and money is in short supply.

A cooperative project with Germany aims to solve the problem. Since 2014 the White City Network has promoted an exchange of know-how, technology and products. In May 2015, a centre for the protection of buildings was inaugurated with an exhibition by students of the Bauhaus University in Weimar. It is a focal point for the cooperation, which is not intended to be one-sided development aid but a true partnership. Apart from being a forum for dialogue between experts, the centre aims to communicate the architectural heritage of the White City to citizens of Tel Aviv and tourists.

The Max Liebling House, built by Dov Karmi in 1936 for the businessman of that name, is a suitable place for this. Karmi, one of the city's most important architects, was born in Ukraine and came to Palestine at the age of 16. He studied architecture in Belgium, from where he brought the International Modern style back to Tel Aviv.

Address Idelson Street 29, Tel Aviv – City Centre | Getting there Bus 3, 17, 19, 22 or 31 to Allenby/Yona haNavi, in the opposite direction to Allenby/Geula | Hours At present only open for events. The internet site is under construction. Contact tourist information: visittelavivyafo@gmail.com, +972 (3) 5166188 | Tip It is only a few paces to the historic city centre with the former city hall, Beit haIr, now a museum of the history of Tel Aviv, and Beit Bialik, home of the great Hebrew national poet, who spent his last nine years here.

# 105 The Window onto the Boulevard

*Art for sitting on*

On Rothschild Boulevard, at the crossroads with little Shadal Street, a green chair stands on a pyramidal plinth in the pedestrian zone. *Window onto the Boulevard* is the name of this sculpture by Buky Schwartz, an Israeli artist who died in 2009 and who was best known for his painted steel sculptures. You will discover the second element of the work when you sit on the chair, because then your gaze will take in the other side of the street, where a yellow steel structure stands. On closer inspection, it turns out to be a window with blue curtains.

Schwartz was born in 1932 in Jerusalem. He studied under Yitzhak Danziger (see ch. 28) at the Avni Institute for Art and Design in Tel Aviv, and also in London at St Martin's School of Art, where he later taught briefly. In addition to his steel sculptures, which can be found in many public places in Israel, he gained international recognition for his video works. The sculpture on Rothschild Boulevard is a popular photo motif. Sometimes, especially at weekends, you have to join a queue to sit on the chair. Once you are in position, it is a wonderful spot from which to let your gaze and your thoughts roam. On this, the city's first boulevard, built in the sand, stand several of the finest buildings in Tel Aviv. The large building on the other side of the street, for example: constructed in 1924 in the eclectic style, it accommodated the embassy of the Soviet Union after the foundation of the state of Israel. In February 1953, Jewish extremists threw a bomb at it in protest against the persecution of Jews in the USSR. This caused the Soviet Union to break off diplomatic relations with Israel.

From the green chair you can, of course, also look across to Max Brenner, which lies opposite. If you do so, then it is time to take some calories on board, as Max Brenner sells the best chocolate in Israel.

**Address** Corner of Sderot Rothschild and Shadal, Tel Aviv – City Centre | Getting there Bus 5 or 142 to Rothschild / Nachmani, bus 70 to haBursa / Rothschild | Tip At the other end of Shadal Street is the underground bar Radio EPGB, one of the hippest clubs in the city, a venue for inditronica and underground music.

# 106__Yael Street
*A small street with large buildings*

A particularly fine concentration of buildings in the International Modern style, forming Tel Aviv's White City, lies around small, quiet Yael Street. It starts with the Dunkelblum House (number 3), an imposing dwelling that was built by Oskar Kaufmann for a lawyer, later a judge at the supreme court, named Menachem Dunkelblum. Kaufmann, born in Hungary and trained as an architect in Karlsruhe in Germany, was a specialist for building theatres who lived and worked in Berlin. A commission to build a theatre for the haBimah ensemble brought him to Tel Aviv in summer 1933. The house in Yael Street is also a little bit reminiscent of a theatre. A balcony with steps leading up at the sides has been placed above the entrance like a little stage. The unusual curved shapes of the windows are also remarkable. The International Modern style was adapted to the climate in Tel Aviv, a fact that can be observed here on, for example, the balconies whose clean lines are interrupted by a grille for ventilation. The Rosenwasser House (number 5) also diverges from the usual European standards: here the architects, Yehuda Fogel and Shlomo Mokeri, put slits along the entire length of the balconies. Bull's-eye windows, which like the brown tiles around the entrance were directly imported from Germany, ventilate the stairwells.

A lot of building materials came to Palestine as a result of the so-called Haavara Agreement, which the Jewish Agency concluded with the German Ministry of the Economy in order to enable Jewish emigrants to transfer at least part of their assets to Palestine. In return for this, German goods were purchased and used to build houses, among other things. The house at number 4 Ruth Street also benefited from this arrangement. From the outside you can admire, for example, a beautiful original wooden letter box that dates from the 1930s.

**Address** Yael Street, between Shulamit and Shlomo haMelech Street, Tel Aviv – Old North | **Getting there** Bus 5, 39, 61 or 72 to Kikar Dizengoff / Dizengoff, in the opposite direction to Beit Lessin / Dizengoff, then across Dizengoff Square and along Zamenhoff Street and Shulamit Street | **Tip** Cafelix from the Noga quarter (see ch. 71) has a branch just round the corner at no. 12 Shlomo haMelech Street, where you can enjoy the superb coffee from this bean roaster on a balcony on the upper ground floor of a Bauhaus building.

# 107__Yafa
*A dialogue of cultures through literature*

A bookshop in Jaffa, and, it should be noted, one that sells books in Arabic – there was no such thing 15 years ago, although Jaffa has some 17,000 Arab residents today. In the past, anyone who wanted to buy literature in Arabic had to travel to Jerusalem or Haifa. In Ramle, where Michel El-Raheb grew up, and in Jaffa it was not available. Michel's love of literature combined with Dina Lee's wish to create a place for dialogue and mutual understanding, and this was the genesis of Yafa. In 2003, a Christian Arab man and a Jewish woman together opened this bookshop, which is also a café.

Arabic literature is sold here in the original version and in Hebrew and English translations, as well as books about the conflict in the Middle East and the Arab world in general. You can also take a seat in the cosy café, where turquoise is the dominant colour, to enjoy a good selection of simple meals, a mixture of Arab food and the Tel Aviv coffee-house style, while browsing in books. Although it was opened in the middle of the Second Intifada, Yafa quickly became a well-attended arts centre that held film evenings, book presentations and talks. Dina Lee passed away in 2012, but the partnership had already broken up. Michel continues to run Yafa.

Today, Yafa holds language courses in Arabic and workshops, but the number of events has declined. Nevertheless, it is a good place for getting to know Arab culture. Michel is usually present himself and willing to talk.

The question of whether Arab intellectual life in Jaffa has been given an impetus again, which was once Michel's vision, cannot be answered so easily. Yafa remains an island. This is also true in respect of its role as a place for encounters, as of course only people who are open for a dialogue are interested in coming here. In spite of this, it is worth paying a visit to this island.

**Address** Yehuda haMargoza Street 33, Tel Aviv – Jaffa North, www.yafabook.co.il |
**Getting there** Bus 10 to Yefet / Louis Pasteur, bus 37 to Yehuda Margoza / Yefet |
**Hours** Sun – Thu 8am – 11pm, Fri 8am – 6pm, Sat 10.30am – 11pm | **Tip** A little further
up Yefet Street stands St Anthony's, a Catholic church where Mass is held daily in
English and Arabic (www.jaffatsparish.com).

# 108__ The Yarkon Bridge

*Parakeets at sundown*

It is difficult to imagine today that the bridge across the river Yarkon, where the road Derech Namir now runs, was still the biggest bridge in the whole country in the 1950s. Its origins are back in World War I, when British troops spanned the Yarkon with a pontoon bridge. This was not replaced with a concrete bridge until 1927. After 1948, the increasing volume of traffic exceeded its capacity, as Tel Aviv grew out to the north and new residential areas such as Ramat Aviv were connected to the inner city via the bridge.

In 1958, a new bridge was finally opened. To this day it has retained its characteristic feature, the tall arches of steel. In the 1950s they were regarded as a symbol of the modern city. The bridge was mentioned in a variety of cultural contexts. It gave its name to the Gesher-ha Yarkon Trio, which only existed for two years, between 1964 and 1966, but was extremely well known because of its members, Arik Einstein, Yehoram Gaon and Beni Amdursky. The bridge was also the subject of a legendary sketch in the popular television show *Sehu se*. People feel the need to take possession of a genuine symbol like this, which is why Tel Aviv's motorcyclists rode on the bridge's steel arches in daring manoeuvres that the police were not easily able to prevent.

In the 1970s the bridge was widened once again and a small, lower-lying pedestrian crossing was added to it. From here, sheltered a little from the noise of the road, you have a wonderful view of the river and can watch the sun go down. At weekends, especially, a lot of boats are on the move, and in the summer months you can enjoy a remarkable spectacle: with a great deal of screeching, swarms of green birds, ring-necked parakeets, thousands of which live wild in Yarkon Park, fly to their roosts for the night, the big eucalyptus trees by the river.

Address Derech Namir between Bnei Dan Street and Sderot Rokach, Tel Aviv – New North | Getting there Bus 22, 25, 45 or 89 to Derech Namir / Yehuda haMaccabi | Tip On Friday afternoons, players of the A.S.A. Tel Aviv Rugby Club train on the field between the bridge and Sportek. At weekends, matches are often played here, free for spectators.

# 109 Yehuda haLevy Street

*Between Ahuzat Bait and the financial district*

Nowhere can you trace the evolution of Tel Aviv as clearly as on a walk along Yehuda haLevy Street. It takes its name from the important poet, philosopher and physician Rav Yehuda haLevy, who lived in medieval Spain. The street runs almost two kilometres from Neve Tzedek to Ibn Gvirol Street, linking up various chapters in city history. 'My heart is in the east, and yet I am in the utmost west,' wrote Yehuda haLevy. He was referring to Jerusalem and Spain, but this quote perfectly fits what was once the longest street in Tel Aviv.

The best course is to start the walk in Neve Tzedek and head north along the street. The first building ever in Tel Aviv was constructed here, at number 25 Yehuda haLevy Street, only a few months after lots were drawn for the plots of land of the Ahuzat Bait community. Unfortunately, it was demolished in the 1960s. Yehuda haLevy Street was one of the first five to be built in Tel Aviv and at the same time the southernmost of the Ahuzat Bait community. Behind it ran the railway connecting Jaffa with Jerusalem, but it is hard to imagine that today. The section that follows is characterised by a strange mix of two-storey buildings dating from the 1920s and office high-rises with mirror-glass façades. The street is also a synonym for the banking sector in Israel, as the three major banks, Hapoalim, Leumi and Discount, have established their headquarters here. At the crossroads with haRakevet Street, where the rail tracks ran in a curve, there was a station until 1970. It was later a terminus, and was called Tel Aviv South. The next part of the street is lined by many buildings in the International Modern style, though not all of them have been restored. The course of Yehuda haLevy Street runs parallel to Rothschild Boulevard as far as Ibn Gvirol Street, the southern part of which was still part of Yehuda haLevy in the 1950s.

Address Yehuda haLevy Street, starting from Pines Street, Tel Aviv – Neve Tzedek |
Getting there Bus 40 or 41 to Eilat/Shlush | Tip Near the junction with Lincoln
Street, where the Survey of Israel offices occupy a building with a heritage listing, a
new park with an ecological pond was recently created. It is a marvellous little refuge
in a densely built-up quarter.

# 110_ The Zamenhof Clinic
*The heart of the health service*

In spring 2012, an era ended – the era of the Zamenhof Clinic. For more than 75 years Zamenhof Street, which runs off King George Street, was home to the central clinic of the health insurance service, Kupat Holim Clalit. 'I have to go to the Zamenhof' – this became a standard expression for going to the doctor. The clinic was built between 1934 and 1936 on agricultural land in the International Modern style that was then fashionable: a plain-looking structure with windows in rows, no balconies and rounded corners, smooth and simple. Later it was extended so that the premises had a total area of 4,700 square metres.

For many decades the Zamenhof was one of the principal clinics of Kupat Holim Clalit. Many consultant doctors were housed here, as well as emergency services. For a long time it was also the most modern facility operated by the health service. At the start of the 20th century there was not yet a comprehensive system of health care in Palestine. In 1909, the year when Tel Aviv was founded, there were no more than 27 Jewish doctors in the whole country. It was only through the immigration of German Jewish doctors that disciplines like X-ray medicine, orthopaedics and so on were established in Palestine, and a revolution in health care began. At Zamenhof, too, many German doctors were active.

The good old days are long gone at the central clinic, however, and the building no longer meets modern standards. In 2005, the decision was taken to close the Zamenhof, sell it and reallocate its various departments to other large medical practices. As the city authorities have designated the building as worth retaining, the real-estate developer that converted the site into 50 apartments was required to leave the west façade standing, so that at least an impressive architectural reminder remains of what was once the central clinic.

Address Corner of Zamenhof Street and Shimshon haGibor, Tel Aviv – Old North |
Getting there Bus 18, 25, 38 or 82 to haMelech George / Zamenhoff / Kikar Masaryk |
Tip In the west of Zamenhof Street, which is named after the inventor of Esperanto,
the Russian Jew Ludwik Leizer Zamenhof, some Bauhaus architecture can be seen. The
street ends at Kikar Dizengoff next to the beautifully restored Cinema Hotel, once the
home of the Esther Cinema. It is worth taking a look inside the lobby.

# 111 Zionism Boulevard

*A walk past villas*

If you ask for directions to Sderot haZionut, the reaction will usually be a puzzled expression. Zionism Boulevard is not really a boulevard but a relatively short stretch of street about 100 metres long with only a traffic island, usually hemmed in by parked cars, at its centre. There is no boulevard atmosphere here. Its continuation from Moshe Sharett Street onwards is only a small footpath surrounded by pleasant greenery. But in fact, in the 1970s it was intended to become a boulevard, and a really long one at that, between Jabotinsky Street and Pincas Street, which gives access to the new residential quarters to the north. However, residents of the Zameret neighbourhood successfully protested against these plans. The street was cut off and turned into a small park.

This was fortunate, because the park is one of the most attractive in the north of the city, always quiet and tidy, always worth a visit. The path winds through the hilly terrain, passing a small playground, benches and trees and continuing to Ahavat Zion Street, where the footpath (and therefore Zionism Boulevard too) comes to an end. The playground, which was beautifully renovated a few years ago, is mainly used by the people who live in the immediate neighbourhood, because many people do not notice the small park, which runs parallel to the streets.

The best way back is to walk through the Zameret quarter, for example along Akiba Arie Street, which takes its name from Akiba Arie Weiss, one of the founders of the city. Here and there in small side streets that come to a dead end you will find the finest villas in Tel Aviv. Each of them is special, each one expensive and luxurious but not ostentatious. Zameret is one of the most expensive places to live in the whole of Israel. Although high walls conceal a few of the houses, this area has preserved a neighbourly character.

**Address** Corner of Sderot haZionut and Jabotinsky to Ahavat Zion Street, Tel Aviv – New North | **Getting there** Bus 22 to Jabotinsky/Derech Namir, bus 7, 14, 66 or 89 to Weizmann/Kikar haMedina | **Tip** By walking along Pincas Street, at the end of the boulevard you go east to Zamaret Park, where twelve high-rise blocks with luxury flats have been built in recent years. In the shopping centre there you can enjoy coffee and cakes in suitably high quality at Celia and Reviva.

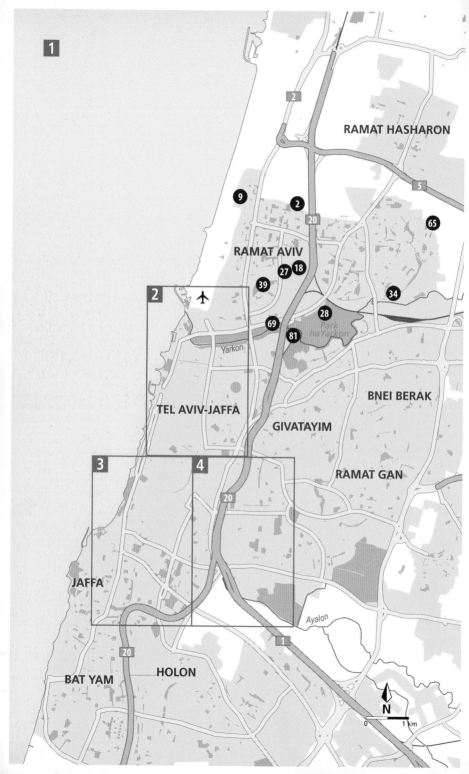

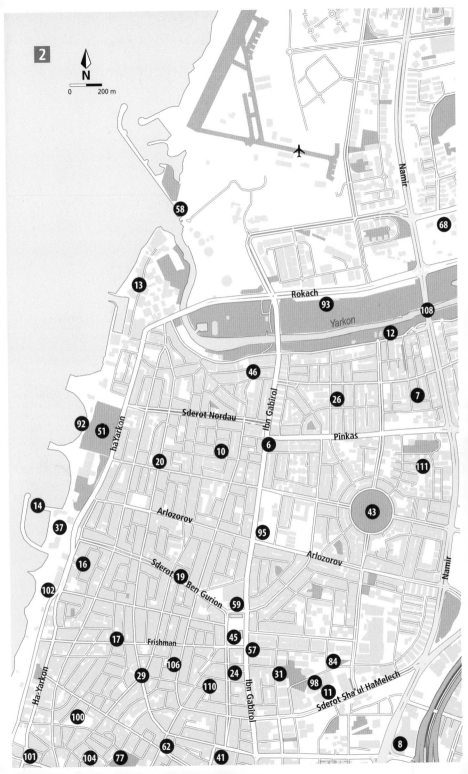

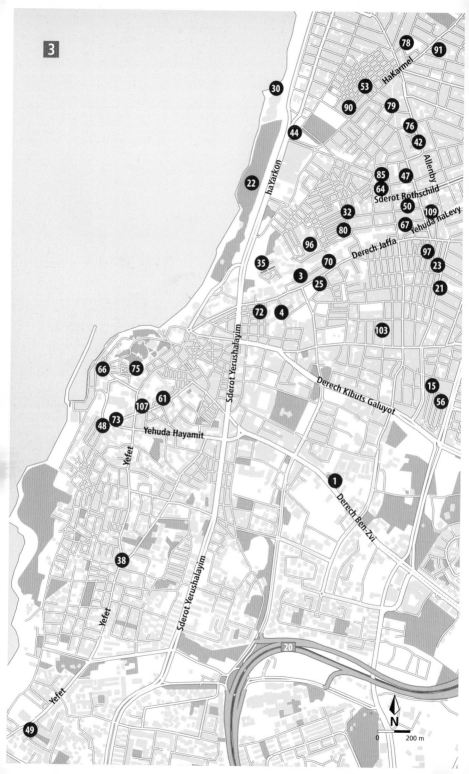

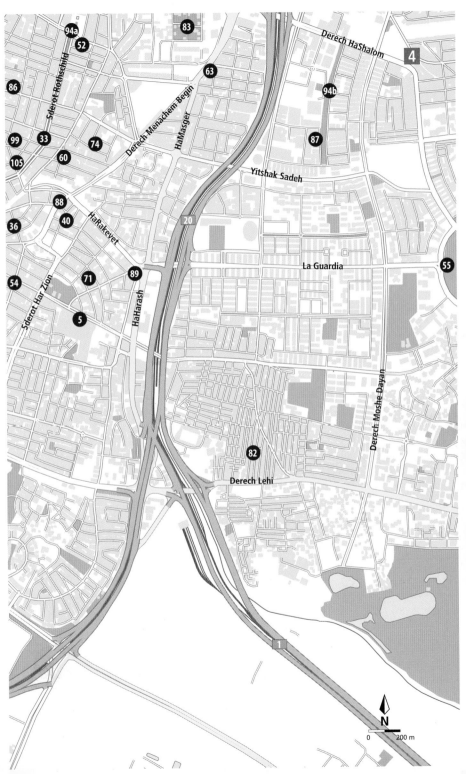

Lucia Jay von Seldeneck,
Carolin Huder, Verena Eidel
**111 PLACES IN BERLIN
THAT YOU SHOULDN'T MISS**
ISBN 978-3-95451-208-9

Rüdiger Liedtke
**111 PLACES IN MUNICH
THAT YOU SHOULDN'T MISS**
ISBN 978-3-95451-222-5

Frank McNally
**111 PLACES IN DUBLIN
THAT YOU SHOULDN'T MISS**
ISBN 978-3-95451-649-0

Rike Wolf
**111 PLACES IN HAMBURG
THAT YOU SHOULDN'T MISS**
ISBN 978-3-95451-234-8

Paul Kohl
**111 PLACES IN BERLIN
ON THE TRAIL OF THE NAZIS**
ISBN 978-3-95451-323-9

Peter Eickhoff
**111 PLACES IN VIENNA
THAT YOU SHOULDN'T MISS**
ISBN 978-3-95451-206-5

Sharon Fernandes
**111 PLACES IN NEW DELHI
THAT YOU MUST NOT MISS**
ISBN 978-3-95451-648-3

Sally Asher, Michael Murphy
**111 PLACES IN NEW ORLEANS
THAT YOU MUST NOT MISS**
ISBN 978-3-95451-645-2

Gordon Streisand
**111 PLACES IN MIAMI
AND THE KEYS
THAT YOU MUST NOT MISS**
ISBN 978-3-95451-644-5

Dirk Engelhardt
**111 PLACES IN BARCELONA
THAT YOU MUST NOT MISS**
ISBN 978-3-95451-353-6

Rüdiger Liedtke
**111 PLACES ON MALLORCA
THAT YOU SHOULDN'T MISS**
ISBN 978-3-95451-281-2

Marcus X. Schmid
**111 PLACES IN ISTANBUL
THAT YOU MUST NOT MISS**
ISBN 978-3-95451-423-6

Stefan Spath
**111 PLACES IN SALZBURG
THAT YOU SHOULDN'T MISS**
ISBN 978-3-95451-230-0

Ralf Nestmeyer
**111 PLACES IN PROVENCE
THAT YOU MUST NOT MISS**
ISBN 978-3-95451-422-9

Christiane Bröcker,
Babette Schröder
**111 PLACES IN STOCKHOLM
THAT YOU MUST NOT MISS**
ISBN 978-3-95451-459-5

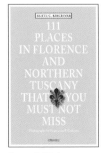

Beate C. Kirchner
**111 PLACES IN FLORENCE
AND NORTHERN TUSCANY
THAT YOU MUST NOT MISS**
ISBN 978-3-95451-613-1

Floriana Petersen, Steve Werney
**111 PLACES IN SAN FRANCISCO
THAT YOU MUST NOT MISS**
ISBN 978-3-95451-609-4

Ralf Nestmeyer
**111 PLACES ON THE
FRENCH RIVIERA
THAT YOU MUST NOT MISS**
ISBN 978-3-95451-612-4

Gerd Wolfgang Sievers
**111 PLACES IN VENICE**
**THAT YOU MUST NOT MISS**
ISBN 978-3-95451-460-1

Petra Sophia Zimmermann
**111 PLACES IN VERONA**
**AND LAKE GARDA THAT**
**YOU MUST NOT MISS**
ISBN 978-3-95451-611-7

Rüdiger Liedtke,
Laszlo Trankovits
**111 PLACES IN CAPE TOWN**
**THAT YOU MUST NOT MISS**
ISBN 978-3-95451-610-0

Gillian Tait
**111 PLACES IN EDINBURGH**
**THAT YOU SHOULDN'T MISS**
ISBN 978-3-95451-883-8

Laurel Moglen, Julia Posey
**111 PLACES IN LOS ANGELES**
**THAT YOU SHOULDN'T MISS**
ISBN 978-3-95451-884-5

Beate C. Kirchner
**111 PLACES IN RIO**
**DE JANEIRO THAT**
**YOU MUST NOT MISS**
ISBN 978-3-7408-0262-2

John Sykes
**111 PLACES IN LONDON**
**THAT YOU SHOULDN'T MISS**
ISBN 978-3-95451-346-8

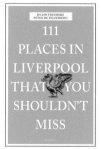

Julian Treuherz,
Peter de Figueiredo
**111 PLACES IN LIVERPOOL**
**THAT YOU SHOULDN'T MISS**
ISBN 978-3-95451-769-5

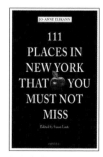

Jo-Anne Elikann
**111 PLACES IN NEW YORK**
**THAT YOU MUST NOT MISS**
ISBN 978-3-95451-052-8

Matěj Černý, Marie Peřinová
**111 PLACES IN PRAGUE
THAT YOU SHOULDN'T MISS**
ISBN 978-3-7408-0144-1

Sybil Canac, Renée Grimaud,
Katia Thomas
**111 PLACES IN PARIS THAT
YOU SHOULDN'T MISS**
ISBN 978-3-7408-0159-5

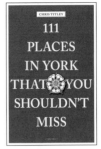

Chris Titley
**111 PLACES IN YORK THAT
YOU SHOULDN'T MISS**
ISBN 978-3-95451-768-8

Kathrin Bielfeldt,
Raymond Wong, Jürgen Bürger
**111 PLACES IN HONG KONG
THAT YOU SHOULDN'T MISS**
ISBN 978-3-95451-936-1

Justin Postlethwaite
**111 PLACES IN BATH THAT
YOU SHOULDN'T MISS**
ISBN 978-3-7408-0146-5

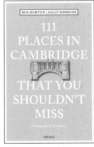

Rosalind Horton,
Sally Simmons, Guy Snape
**111 PLACES IN CAMBRIDGE
THAT YOU SHOULDN'T MISS**
ISBN 978-3-7408-0147-2

Joe DiStefano, Clay Williams
**111 PLACES IN QUEENS
THAT YOU MUST NOT MISS**
ISBN 978-3-7408-0020-8

Allison Robicelli, John Dean
**111 PLACES IN BALTIMORE
THAT YOU MUST NOT MISS**
ISBN 978-3-7408-0158-8

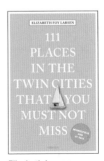

Elisabeth Larsen
**111 PLACES IN THE
TWIN CITIES THAT
YOU MUST NOT MISS**
ISBN 978-3-7408-0029-1

**07/18/18**

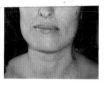

**Andrea Livnat,** who was born in 1974 and grew up in Munich, is a historian, journalist and editor-in-chief of the Jewish internet service haGalil. She has lived in Tel Aviv since her dissertation took her there 13 years ago, and is glad almost every day that her children are growing up in the city.

*The photographer*

**Angelika Baumgartner** is an interior designer from Munich who loves to travel and take photographs. In Tel Aviv she is delighted by all aspects of the city and has fallen in love with the beach, from the old port in Jaffa to the new harbour in the north of the city.